RETHINKING
LUXURY

MARTIN C. WITTIG
FABIAN SOMMERROCK
PHILIP BEIL
MARKUS ALBERS

RETHINKING
LUXURY

HOW TO MARKET EXCLUSIVE
PRODUCTS AND SERVICES IN AN
EVER-CHANGING ENVIRONMENT

Roland Berger
Strategy Consultants

Published by
LID Publishing Ltd
The Loft, 19a Floral Street, Covent Garden, London WC2E 9DS
United Kingdom
info@lidpublishing.com
www.lidpublishing.com

A member of: **BPR** ⚙

Business Publishers Roundtable

www.businesspublishersroundtable.com

Printed in Spain by COFAS S.A.
ISBN: 978-1-907794-56-8

Conception and Realisation
Rethink GmbH, Hegelplatz 1, 10117 Berlin

rethink

Creative Team
Brian O'Connor, Suvi Häring, Elisabeth Moch, Vera Müller,
Anne Schälike, Maria Thiele, Frank Zinsmeister

Editorial Team
Andrew Bulkeley, Kevin Cote, Axel Hansen, Anthony Heric,
Stefan Kesselhut, Jörn Kengelbach, Aimee Male, Dave Rimmer, Katrin Seegers,
Barbara Serfozo, Marlene Sørensen, Lisa Wicklund, Ralf Wildung

Project Management
Sarah Broßeder, Andrea Schumacher

Lithography
Twentyfour Seven GmbH

CONTENTS

WHY WE WROTE THIS BOOK

RETHINKING LUXURY

The luxury industry has
been hesitant to admit the world
is changing. That's because
it was long a market governed
by tradition and firmly
based in Europe's old world aura.
But the rapid pace of innovation
and demographic upheaval
has made even the most staid
luxury company take note.
And this is only the beginning.

Shifts in demographics, money flows and values mean luxury consumers are becoming more digital and more interested in sustainability. They are also more Asian, with cultural backgrounds that are often alien to traditional makers of luxury products and services in Europe. Today's luxury consumer still longs for purchases that are steeped in European tradition and craftsmanship, but there are signs that this is changing.

The future of superlative products remains based in tradition, but non-traditional things such as smartphones, the Internet and social media are influencing it. Companies can now embrace the power of digital technology to lure the most high-paying customers and increase customer loyalty with carefully crafted offers of exclusivity. To do this, they enlist the help of carefully tended databases that include sales histories and clues about what the customer finds interesting on the company's website. Today, a blogger can be more important to a luxury brand than any of the traditional "gatekeepers". For companies such as Burberry, communicating digitally with their customers is at least as important as opening a shiny new flagship store in London.

At the same time, sustainability is becoming more and more important because a new breed of customer is asking questions about ethics and the environment. Some Gucci handbags already come with a "passport" detailing the history of the leather it was made from – Gucci only sources leather for its bags from approved ranches in Brazil. The company says it is acknowledging that its customers are changing, and that they now want to know the origin of materials and how products are made.

In addition to the digital revolution and concerns about sustainability, the rise of China and other Asian economies is changing the way luxury brands and their marketers operate. The United States remains the biggest luxury market, but influences are increasingly Asian. Pop culture can now come from Gangnam, Seoul, as well as from the streets of Brooklyn. China is the fastest-growing market for luxury products, and it is only a matter of time before it becomes the nation with the largest number of purchasers of upmarket goods. And in India, the number of millionaires jumped by 22 per cent in 2012.

Asia, values and digital technology are all parts of the future of the luxury industry. But what does this mean for managers and marketers? What's the best way to do business in China? How do you make sure customers talk about your sustainable products? Should you invite bloggers rather than magazine journalists to your next runway show? Do you need more retail locations, or should you focus on e-commerce? How do you engage the next generation of critical, informed and digital-savvy customers, and turn them into loyal customers?

To find answers, we looked at the latest studies and analysed broad industry trends as well as specific micro trends. We also conducted in-depth interviews with company heads and opinion leaders in the luxury industry itself. They told us their views on the changing landscape of their business, and which strategies they plan to implement. The exclusive interviews also revealed which trends inspire these executives and which ones frighten them. *Rethinking Luxury* will help retailers cope with the rise of digital technology. It will provide luxury hotels with information to update the services they provide to guests, and it will show everyone how big data can be harnessed to improve service and sales.

First, we define the market and what we mean by "luxury". In the second chapter, "The Evolving Face of Luxury", we deal with the new and established demands of luxury customers. Here, we show why old stereotypes of target groups no longer hold today, and how new types of consumers can be identified and reached. Then we introduce trends that we feel are driving the future of this particular business. In the third chapter, "East is the New West", we analyse a tectonic shift that is moving the luxury industry's core market to Asia, and identify successful strategies to deal with it. The fourth chapter, "Is Bling No Longer King?", deals with the rise of values and the need for sophisticated storytelling in developed luxury markets as well as qualified responses to this trend. In the fifth chapter, "The New Age of Access", we talk about the astonishing rise of digital communication platforms and online retail. Again, we identify key takeaways for successfully managing this transition. In "What's in Store for Stationary Retail?", chapter six, we show how the world of bricks and mortar can remain sexy in an increasingly digital world, and how it can even become more relevant.

Chapter seven, "The Luxury Experience", is a wake-up call for anyone who believes that luxury can exist as a physical entity only. We discuss services and non-physical products as well as how to create new ecosystems of experience around existing products. Chapter eight is all about considered consumption as the new indulgence. We show how it is possible to enjoy products while supporting sustainability. We encourage brands to embrace sustainability not just as a stylish way of greenwashing but also as a serious rethinking of all processes in the supply chain. Because we envision an end to pure hedonism and the rise of the critical consumer, we strongly believe in the ability of luxury brands to position themselves as the first providers of authentic sustainability.

Finally, in chapter nine, we tie it all together. This culminates in the one question that should concern every CEO and marketer of luxury brands today: How can we make customers choose us over our competitors time and time again, even as digital communication gives customers total transparency in prices, trends, quality and production? How can marketers maintain loyalty when people have multiple options?

It's time to rethink what luxury means today, and will mean in the future.

We have combined market research with probing interviews with people at the heart of the luxury business. We've included our own analysis and prognoses. Still, we see *Rethinking Luxury* as a starting place and a resource. We would like to continue this debate with you. To engage, just visit our website, www.rolandberger.com/rethinking-luxury, or follow us on Twitter (@rethinkluxury, @BergerNews).

Thank you.

Martin C. Wittig
Fabian Sommerrock
Philip Beil
Markus Albers

CHAPTER ONE

THE STATE OF LUXURY

Theories and definitions for
superlative goods in an
ever-changing marketplace

RETHINKING LUXURY

Clear definitions of luxury are rare,
but most agree that you know
it when you see it. Luxury is as much
about the story and mystique
surrounding the product as it is about
the product itself. A high price and
scarcity are not the only components
of luxury. Consumers need to
be buying into a story or history.
A watch can rely on mechanical
works developed over a century ago
that are impossible to replicate
with computers and lasers today.
Entire generations may have
fretted over the perfect stitching
and leather for a shoe.

Many define luxury as almost anything that is not essential. "Some people think that luxury is the opposite of poverty. It's not. Luxury is the opposite of vulgarity," as Coco Chanel famously remarked. She defined luxury as a coat with a silk or fur lining that only the owner knows about. Luxury consumers express themselves and show their self-image through their purchases. Someone who buys a single watch, a single super-luxury car or goes on a once-in-a-lifetime trip clearly knows what they want. They are displaying their ability to afford that product or service, and showing everyone that they have made a conscious selection.

Luxury is curated. Luxury is for connoisseurs. It is not only the price that makes a product luxurious. Its attributes do as well. Everything about a luxury product or service should cater to those who know why a luxury product is what it is, and how it came to be. Luxury products are exceptional from concept to realisation. They have superlative attributes. Aluminium or steel should not be used in place of titanium. An unthinking robot should not replace a trained, passionate craftsman. Luxury is not about cost, but is about demanding and owning something exceptional. Those attributes, to some degree, should contribute to the price.

Many raw materials carry hefty price tags because they are either rare or difficult to obtain. Many luxury items are not primarily about the most expensive materials. They are manufactured using exactly the right materials for the job: leather from a specific breed of animal, the ideal metal, a little-used oil. The materials are then assembled by artisans who are even more passionate about the items than their purchasers. These are craftsmen who often work with the same tools that have been used for decades. If they use more modern tools, they have good reason to do so and can explain why the new technology leads to a superior product.

This is what defines luxury and distinguishes it from premium or even mass-market brands. Luxury products are, at least in theory, the very best a product can possibly be. And that means they tend to take time and resources to produce, creating a scarcity of supply and exclusivity of ownership. Also, luxury contains many grey areas that obscure an objective definition. Luxury is subjective and relative, and involves a range of immaterial aspects. And that is exactly the way it should be. Luxury is, and always will be, deeply individual. The infographic on pages 18 and 19 helps illuminate the differences between premium and luxury goods.

LUXURY STORIES

Compelling stories, more than mere facts, convey a certain passion, a sensuality that brings the product to life for the buyer. Luxury products spark emotion, offering more than indulgence. These emotions are based on the soul of a product, its story. This is why there is a terrific story behind almost all luxury brands.

Patek Philippe watches are an excellent example. The company's history goes back to 1839, when Antoine Norbert de Patek began making watches in Geneva. At the time, Patek was just doing what craftsmen in Geneva did best, which was making watches. The company's story is therefore tied to more than just its own history. It is also tied to Geneva's history and Switzerland's past. Jean Adrien Philippe joined in 1851, and the company has made watches ever since. While ownership changed hands in the early 20th century, the importance of tradition was not lost. If you are a Patek Philippe owner, you already know all this. That is the point. You have not bought just a watch, you have also bought a tiny piece of Switzerland along with the technology and timeless design.

This does not mean luxury products cannot evolve or change. They can, and often do, embrace the future. But they also must remain faithful to the past. Indeed, luxury products should be shown to grow within the framework of their brand. Think of Hermès, which started selling its famous scarf after being known for decades only for leather goods. And after having excelled at writing instruments, Montblanc added watches and fashion accessories to its portfolio. Or Porsche, which constantly pushes the boundaries of how much technology a car can contain.

A SHORT HISTORY OF LUXURY

Luxury is present in the earliest manifestations of human culture and society. That's because all humans have the same intrinsic needs and desires, and it is our desires that lead to luxury. The definition of luxury has evolved as our needs are satisfied by advancing technology, wealth and hygiene. But people have always wanted a little more than they had before. And they have always coveted rewards for victories. Luxury has always been controversial.

Luxury and affluence can be found in the objects buried in the earliest graves. The first indications are the number and size of items buried along with a body. Some graves are more complex than others from the same time period, and include more items. Graves began not only to include excessive numbers of items, but also individual markings. These markings link the body of the deceased to a specific group, creating a sense of uniqueness. A key component of luxury is this sense of exclusivity.

Luxury was present in the tombs and pyramids of Egypt and played a role in the epic struggle between Athens and the oligarchy of Sparta. A couple of hundred years later in Rome, politicians fretted over conspicuous consumption and passed laws designed to rein in public expressions of wealth.

Sometimes the evolution of seemingly unrelated aspects of life had a surprising impact on luxury. Martin Luther's reformation of the Christian church stirred emotions throughout Europe. In the 16th century, that inspiration arrived in Geneva. Luxury was evident in the outward display of wealth by church leaders and politicians. These people believed God wanted them to surround themselves with luxury, since they were selected by God to be at the top. Geneva played a major role in this opulence since it had many skilled jewellers. However, John Calvin saw these trappings as unnecessary. God did not care about materialism, he argued. Resistance on the part of the wealthy ultimately led to revolution. In the French Revolution and in Switzerland, the people installed politicians more in keeping with Calvin's reformist outlook. Consequently, much

Continued on page 20

The bandwidth of top-level products

Luxury and premium brands differ from each other in the way they are designed and manufactured, as well as in the values they reflect.

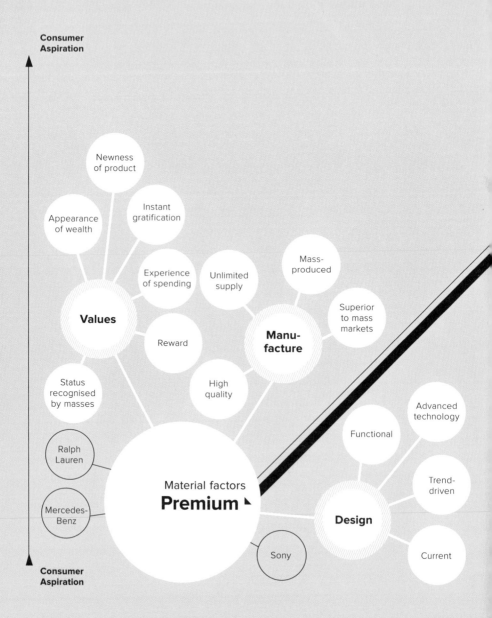

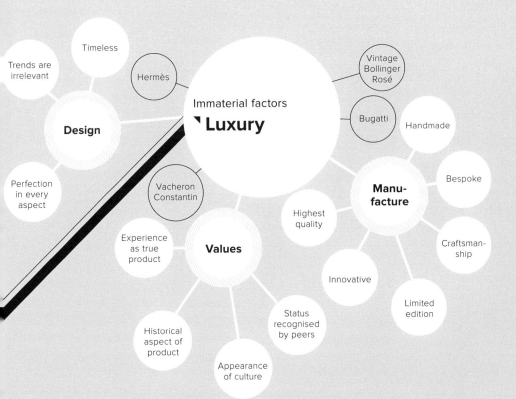

Immaterial factors

Luxury

Timeless

Trends are
irrelevant

Hermès

Design

Perfection
in every
aspect

Vacheron
Constantin

Experience
as true
product

Values

Historical
aspect of
product

Appearance
of culture

Status
recognised
by peers

Highest
quality

Vintage
Bollinger
Rosé

Bugatti

Handmade

**Manu-
facture**

Bespoke

Craftsman-
ship

Innovative

Limited
edition

Source: Roland Berger Strategy Consultants

conspicuous consumption was outlawed and many jewellers were out of a job. It is now widely believed this is the reason Geneva's jewellers, skilled with their hands but lacking an income, moved into watch-making. Switzerland today is synonymous with high-end watchmaking and has a centuries-old tradition that reaches all the way back to Calvin's Geneva.

Later, the unbridled wealth brought on by the Industrial Revolution helped galvanise a sense of luxury. For the first time, aristocrats and merchants were no longer the only consumers able to afford luxury. Plant managers and inventors suddenly also found themselves with the budgets necessary to go luxury shopping, dramatically expanding the market for well-made products. And, as more people moved to the cities to work, Western class systems were simplified. Those at the top end of the middle classes were also able to afford some luxuries.

THE RISE OF LUXURY BRANDS

Early on, luxury was often defined by rare minerals or spices from abroad. The discovery of the New World was in part driven by an attempt to gain easier access to rare spices. But as culture and society matured during the Renaissance and in early modern Europe, so did the concept of luxury. The affluent increasingly wanted rare things, just as aristocrats and royalty had before them, and they wanted these things crafted into exquisite items by artisans – gowns, for example, or extravagant horse coaches. Because of the growing customer base that came with Industrial Revolution and urbanisation, these manufactured products became sought after by much larger groups. As a consequence, in the 20th century the luxury market as we now know it was formed.

Individual manufacturers had worked for monarchs and aristocrats in the past. But now, luxury customers were a market, and a market requires both larger quantities of products and orientation as to which products are suit-able for distinction. That's why luxury became brand-based, as defined by many of the companies and designers we still talk about today.

France's Hermès is an excellent example of how a luxury company evolved based on its strengths. In the early 19th century, founder Thierry Hermès was astonished at the number of horses in Paris. Knowing that good equipment was vital for horse riding, he launched a workshop that crafted saddles and riding gear that were used by the rich and royalty alike. The company created its trademark scarf in the 20th century and added handbags, which would eventually be made famous by Grace Kelly. Adapting its knowledge of leather goods to make inroads into the luxury market, Hermès then became one of the bulwarks of the industry, allowing its products to evolve along with culture. Still, the horse in its trademark reminds everyone of its history. Even if one does not know the history, the Hermés trademark certainly conjures up images of 19th century gentry.

Today there is a variety of luxury companies with differing business models. Three big luxury conglomerates play the largest role in defining modern luxury: LVMH Group, Richemont and Kering (formerly PPR). They offer products from some of the best-known luxury brands, such as LVMH's Louis Vuitton, Richemont's Cartier and Kering's Gucci. LVMH also owns Dom Pérignon Champagne and jeweller Bulgari. Richemont sells Alfred Dunhill products and Jaeger-LeCoultre watches. Kering has Girard-Perregaux watches and Bottega Veneta fashion. And though these conglomerates have been incorporating more and more brands over the years, there are still independent companies, such as Chanel, Ermenegildo Zegna or Brunello Cucinelli. Often they are family run. There are plenty of exceptional porcelain manufacturers, such as Meissen and the Porzellan Manufaktur Nymphenburg in Germany.

In the 1960s, luxury became a darling of the media. There were TV shows about mansions and private jets that showed how the other half lived. In the hedonistic 1980s, everyone yearned for luxury. It was the time of Reaganomics and movies such as Oliver Stone's *Wall Street* – of unbridled fascination with status, brands and logos. Luxury became mainstream and familiar to the masses. But in the 1990s, values and society changed after a world economic crisis. Conspicuous consumption and logo-mania became frowned upon in many Western markets. So luxury evolved to be more about aesthetics and adding that certain something to a consumer's life. Experiences, combined with a product's history, now link the buyer to something greater than the product itself. Because luxury is more than ever associated with expressing one's self, it also reflects divergent lifestyles. Luxury is varied and different for everyone. For proof, just look at the number of luxury brands. And it is difficult to categorise the brands beyond what they produce. Luxury is more than just fashion, watches and jewellery. Luxury covers broad categories, today including many layers of service and, for some, even spirituality. The most common luxury segments today are:

– Fashion and accessories
– Cosmetics and perfume
– Watches and jewellery
– Automobiles
– Wine, champagne and spirits
– Home furnishings
– Yachts
– First-class and private aviation
– Electronics
– Writing instruments
– Art
– Musical instruments
– Hotels
– Restaurants
– Food

We see four distinct business models by which luxury companies operate in these segments. The first is a brand that has its own personality and that makes consumers want to pay above and beyond the product's materials or function. These products are seen as the gold standard of their categories: Montblanc pens, for example. In our second model, products are assembled by true master craftsmen using materials that command a price tag out of reach for most. Bugatti comes to mind. The third relies on investments in patents and technology or by closely following how a product is used. Here Leica cameras are a good example. In our fourth business model, we see companies tightly controlling distribution and requiring consumers to apply in advance to buy their products. Some customers have had to wait years for their Hermès Birkin bag. This way companies create exclusivity and maintain their brand's image, enticing buyers into their often lavish stores for a complete buying experience.

THE LUXURY MARKET

Luxury is relatively immune to swings in economic fortune in comparison to other industries. In the past 15 years, the market for personal luxury goods has more than doubled in size. The market stalled following the stock market crash and the subsequent terrorism attack in New York in 2001, but it did not contract. After catching its breath, the luxury market continued to expand until 2008, when the Lehman Brothers bankruptcy threw global economies into a tailspin. It is little wonder this economic disaster hit the luxury market. It contracted in 2008 and 2009, but only to ricochet in 2010 with 13 per cent growth, and has continued to grow since then, emerging stronger than before the credit crisis. These figures are based on numbers gathered by a study published by the Altagamma Foundation and refer to the personal luxury market, which is essentially items that can be worn, from fashion to watches to perfume. That market is worth more than €200 billion now, but excludes key products such as cars, travel and wine. Folding in those items as well as home furnishings, yachts and food, the market balloons to more than €700 billion but still does not include aviation. And the overall market continues growing dynamically, even when regions such as Japan have problems.

Familial wealth allowed many previous luxury consumers to continue spending through the crisis and, as their portfolios recovered, to expand their outlays as economies also returned to health. Some major shifts are underway in global markets and they, too, helped contribute to the recovery. Fresh millionaires are minted daily in Asia. Economic and demographic shifts are also changing a once-staid luxury market. We discuss these changes in greater detail in chapter three. But suffice it to say, emerging economies are driving growth in spending among the wealthy.

The United States remains the world's biggest luxury market. Among luxury's established, mature markets, Japan, France, Italy, the United Kingdom, Germany and Switzerland are the cornerstones. They are markets we all know. Of the BRIC countries, China and Russia are the ones to watch. Greater China is the second-largest luxury market and will increasingly steal the limelight. Brazil is home to shoppers quite willing to spend on luxury, but the market remains small compared to the segment leaders. India's luxury market is certainly growing, but the country often has its own, unique definition of luxury. Indian customers are unusually fond of local brands, making marketing difficult for international players.

These markets are all set to develop very differently. America's luxury market reflects its reputation as being dynamic and open, and it was the industry's major growth leader in 2013. Europe continues to suffer from the same economic woes that have plagued it for nearly a decade, but with its rich history in luxury, Europe is a popular destination for Asian luxury travellers, and many European markets still have room for growth. Using a yardstick that measures luxury spending against gross domestic product, France and Italy are well above the saturation level, and the German luxury market is currently half of that. This suggests the size limits of a luxury market may also be cultural, not just economic.

It is not surprising that one of the fastest-growing regions for luxury is the Middle East. The region's booming economies have required plenty of foreign assistance, and foreign tastes have come along with it. Coupled with increasing international travel, the luxury market in parts of the Middle East continues to expand. In just a few years, it will have doubled. Still, the Middle East is also suffering from political instability, adding a dose of volatility. Despite recent problems, Brazil will continue to lead the charge in South America where its luxury spending mirrors the growth of its economy. Although it is currently stagnating, Japan is Asia's second-largest luxury market and should be treated as a mature, saturated market.

Luxury has come a long way since its earliest days where it ended in the graves of ancestors. It has evolved along with man and created its own place in our world. While globalisation is making that world smaller, it's also creating new opportunities for luxury brands. This includes sharing formerly regional manufacturing traditions with the entire world, and opening new stores in previously unexplored areas. Europe has traditionally been the epicentre of the luxury world. But that epicentre is slowly moving. In the next chapters, we look more deeply into the evolution of the luxury market and especially at the consumers who define it.

THE HISTORICAL LOOK OF LUXURY

Defining luxury can be difficult. Many argue that they know it when they see it. Here we present a selection of historical items that we feel reflect our ideal of luxury.

1341 – 1323 BCE

Tutankhamun
Luxury has likely been around as long as man.
For historians and archaeologists, graves such as Tutankhamun's
offer clues about past extravagance.

1400

Ming vase

Luxury spending is shifting to Asia but the luxury
market is nothing new to the region. This Ming vase dates
to the 15th century and now sells for millions.

1435 – 1489

Hans Waldmann

Hans Waldmann, a war hero and Zurich mayor,
fought against conspicuous displays of luxury but
failed to act as a role model. His hypocrisy
led to his execution by beheading on April 6, 1489.
This 1937 statue attempts to restore his reputation.

1512

The Sistine Chapel

The Catholic church has always been good
at luxury. Not everyone could hire Michelangelo
as interior decorator.

1600

Harpsichord

Only the wealthy could afford a handmade
instrument as complex as the harpsichord. Many of those
who composed for it were funded by royalty.

1837

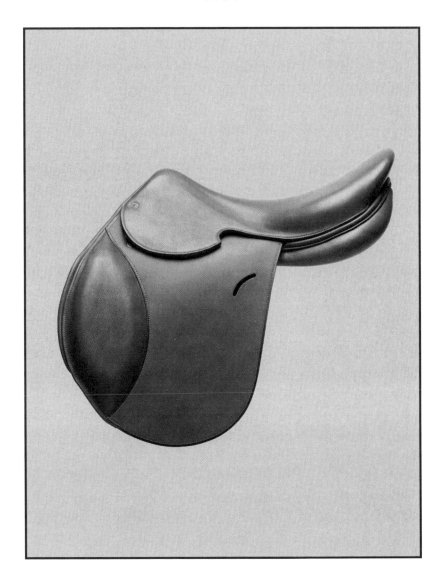

Hermès saddle
Thierry Hermès began
by making tack for Parisians in 1837.
His company still does.

TURN OF THE 20TH CENTURY

Patek Philippe

Switzerland's watchmaking culture arose from the country's
15th-century obsession with eliminating outward signs of wealth.
Bored jewellers began to focus on tourbillons.

1929

Bentley

This Bentley "Birkin Blower" got its name from the
compressor installed on its engine for speed.
It was one of the most advanced cars of its time and
is now part of Ralph Lauren's collection.

1936 – 2008

Yves Saint Laurent
The French fashion icon challenged
social mores and advertising practices while
giving a face to luxury in 1971.

2013

Bernard Arnault
One of the faces of modern luxury is Bernard Arnault,
the CEO who has crafted conglomerate
LVMH as carefully as his artisans craft its products.

"The fragmentation of the luxury market presents considerable opportunities."

An interview with Armando Branchini,
executive director of Fondazione Altagamma,
a foundation promoting Italian luxury brands.

We want to talk about recent developments in luxury marketing and cast a look into the near future. So the first question is: How have the Internet and digital communication changed the way luxury brands engage with their customers?

The breakthrough revolution is that two-way communication between luxury brands and customers is now possible.

Does this mean that the Internet reduces the mystery and exclusivity associated with luxury brands?

As a matter of fact, I believe that entering a traditional bricks-and-mortar store still gives customers the opportunity to experience a brand's philosophy, its identity and its values. Any company offering products and services today of course has to be prepared to communicate properly what constitutes its value proposition. It's difficult to have a value proposition if it's unknown, if it isn't properly communicated. I believe that myth rather than mystery is the appropriate term to use. Myth is the first of the symbolic values of a brand of a company. But you can't sell a luxury product if it's cloaked in mystery.

At the same time, far more people today are talking about luxury, say in the world of fashion blogging.

I believe that this is a sign of maturity and transparency, which is not a trade-off with authenticity. As luxury brands are promising values, it is mandatory for them to be in a position of maintaining such promises. The big challenge of the Internet and social media is the fact that it opens the doors for two-way communication, which has traditionally been in one direction only, from the company to the public. Today, tools such as Twitter, Facebook, YouTube and blogs make customers much more autonomous and independent. This means that they, the customers, play a greater role and can be seen as "prosumers", in the sense that they are not just consumers, but that they are much more concerned and more knowing about products, product comparisons, price comparisons and so on. This is a much more mature market that is challenging the most conservative of the luxury brands. But that gives much more support and potential for growth to those companies that are the best performers in the use of digital tools.

Is it more difficult today to have loyal customers when your competitor is just one mouse click away?

Loyalty is a challenging issue in any case. This is true both for the bricks-and-mortar context as well as for the digital age.

Why have some luxury brands been reluctant to embrace the trend towards digital?

Initially, many companies were in a "wait and see" mode, concerned that the Internet might compromise some traditional luxury values, such as exclusivity and experience. In the last five years, however, two developments occurred. Technology, firstly, created a greater opportunity for the use of multimedia. Rather than simply using drawings or pictures, companies could now use music and movies, for example, to promote events and cultural initiatives. A second and more important factor that occurred in the real rather than in the digital world was a generational shift. The baby boomers, which for 40 years had been the main pillar of consumption for the luxury brands, now account for less than 50 per cent of the overall market. That means, in turn, that more than 50 per cent of customers belong to Generation X and Y. These are much younger customers who are accustomed to using digital tools.

One consequence is that there's an increasing demand for authenticity and transparency. Would you say that one way for luxury brands to approach this is to become even better storytellers? Do you have to tell stories differently on the Internet?

The Internet has indeed generated new opportunities for storytelling. For example, customers were able via web stream to take part in the Fendi fashion show on the Great Wall of China. Another example: the Burberry fashion shows in Milan, which could also be streamed across the world.

Storytelling is not based on technology, but on media. A proliferation of media, in other words, dramatically increases the opportunities for storytelling.

Talking about transparency and authenticity – are luxury brands under pressure today to deliver more sustainable products?

Absolutely. But for me this is unrelated to the Internet. Sustainability has never been a major issue for personal luxury goods. The only concerns in Europe were related to certain industrial phases of woollen fibre products, namely washing, and hide tanning. But from the 1970s, the European Commission issued very strict regulations controlling these activities. It is not correct to perceive of high-luxury brands as companies that endanger the environment.

But doesn't this mean that luxury companies should do a better job at communicating their sustainable behaviour?

I believe that they should consider sustainability to be a given. If you are Gucci, you don't compete with Louis Vuitton, Ferragamo or Chanel on the business of sustainability. You compete on different elements, such as quality or style identity. The final consumer makes his or her choice based on such elements.

How does the emergence of the Chinese and Asian economies change the luxury markets?

China and Asia will remain important pillars of the development of luxury consumption – around 7 per cent of global personal luxury products are purchased in China while about 15 per cent are purchased by Chinese out-side of China, mainly in Europe and the United States. Due to the policies of frugality of the new Chinese president, we see some decline in demand in the domestic market, but final purchases of Chinese customers outside of China are as high as expected. Chinese demand for luxury products has increased significantly, particularly over about the last five years, as people are looking for status. But at the same time, an important part of the finer

The big challenge of the Internet and social media is
the fact that it opens the doors for two-way communication,
from the company to the public.

clientele, who are clever men and women, is truly sophisticated. As such, the learning curve, from "bling-bling" to sophistication, has been much shorter in China than it had been in Russia or even in Japan during the 1970s.

Would you say that there is a general trend towards less conspicuous consumption and more real values?

There is a general trend, which is also happening in the more mature markets. An example would be the success of Bottega Veneta, a company that has never subscribed to "logomania". Having long bought products with the Louis Vuitton or Gucci monogram on them, customers today have become more discerning, looking for sophistication and niche products. This is a structural element in the consumption of superior quality products and services.

Does the typical luxury customer still exist or are target groups becoming increasingly fragmented?

Of course they are increasingly becoming fragmented. Today we assume there are 14 to 16 main profiles of different luxury consumers. In 2012, 50 per cent of purchases in Milan were made by Italian people and the other half by tourists. In Paris and London, only 40 per cent of the purchases were made by locals and the rest by tourists.

In a nutshell, how should brands react to this increasing fragmentation?

If you are a good marketing manager, you are in a position to be able to deal with complexity. The fact that there are so many profiles presents a complication to your life, but it also presents considerable opportunities.

*Having long bought products with the Louis Vuitton
or Gucci monogram on them, customers
today have become more discerning, looking for
sophistication and niche products.*

Luxury brands have always been great about creating experience around their products. Now we increasingly see experience becoming the product.

This is typical of the baby boomers. Rather than being interested in possession, they desire experience. This is strongly related to the curve of their existence: at a younger age, material possessions may play a more central role, while advanced age may encourage alternative preferences. It sometimes takes ages to realise that there is more to luxury than possessing cars or jewels.

Will this become more important in times of economic crisis and increasing pressure for sustainability?

Younger people are still interested in owning. Their time horizons are inclined to years and years of consumption. When the time horizon changes, with age, experience becomes more important.

CHAPTER TWO

THE EVOLVING FACE OF LUXURY

Meeting new and established
customer demands in a
non-homogeneous global market

RETHINKING LUXURY

The streets are similar, and a
similar mix of people visit New York
City's Fifth Avenue, London's
Bond Street and Moscow's
Tretyakovsky Proyezd. There is the
respectable elderly couple
looking at timepieces by Blancpain,
with a design so nondescript it is hard
to see why they are so expensive.
Just beside them, a young millionaire
wearing gold cufflinks pulls up
in his Ferrari, about to buy a new scarf
with a conspicuous Gucci logo.
And across the street, a young
businesswoman dressed in high-street
brands is about to splurge
on a new leather bag from Fendi.

They are all typical luxury consumers – because there is no such thing as a typical luxury consumer. Most people simply do not buy luxury, and those who do share a number of values and habits, but there is a variety of distinct luxury consumer groups that differ from one another in many ways. Many are "occasional" consumers of luxury, making purchases only from time to time, depending on the occasion. But most interesting is the group we call the "real" consumer. Real luxury consumers regularly buy from various product categories, have a profound knowledge about the luxury market and are loyal to trusted brands. There is nothing occasional about their shopping behaviour, because luxury is an integral part of their daily lives. Real consumers know what they are buying. And they know exactly what they want to buy. These luxury customers routinely frequent boutiques, stop by car showrooms and stay at luxury hotels when they are on vacation. However, only a small percentage of the total number of consumers are real luxury consumers – in Germany, for instance, around 3 per cent.

We have already touched on market segmentation in our introduction. But to gain a deeper understanding of the characteristics of real consumers of luxury products – as opposed to occasional consumers – we need to gain a deeper understanding of them. How do real luxury consumers differ from one another? In answering this question, we can use our consumer-related insights as a basis for marketing and management decisions.

FOUR TARGET GROUPS AND THE CONTINUUM OF MATURITY

Real consumers are not a homogeneous group. We have identified four subgroups: "Newcomers", "Climbers", "Exclusivity Enthusiasts" and "True Connoisseurs". They are similiar because they are all avid buyers of luxury items, yet they buy for different reasons. Instead of starting with socio-demographic categories, like most consumer typologies, the following typology is based on the buying behaviour of consumers and their general stance on luxury. One of the central findings is that there is a difference when it comes to the average age of the typical buyer of certain luxury brands. This is the Continuum of Maturity. The Newcomers are the youngest group, just starting to acquire luxury items. As we will see, their buying behaviour and attitudes are very different from older and more affluent Climbers and Exclusivity Enthusiasts, and especially True Connoisseurs, the oldest and wealthiest group.

We are also seeing that the overall number of luxury consumers, real and occasional, has grown considerably. Luxury markets are thriving, and not just in emerging markets such as China and Russia, but also in mature ones like Germany, where the market for luxury products grew by 16 per cent in 2011. For a more comprehensive insight into all four luxury consumer groups, let's meet someone from each group.

NEWCOMER: WHAT YOU HAVE IS WHAT YOU ARE

Meet Lisa. She is 33 years old, and wants to stand out in a crowd. After getting home from work she loves sitting at her kitchen table and reading *Cosmopolitan*. She gets most of her inspiration for shopping trips from looking at celebrities and the latest fashion trends. When she buys luxury items, she wants others to see what she can afford, so she tends to buy items which promise to give her higher social status. Identifiable items and logos are more important to her than the tradition and heritage of a brand, the workmanship of a product or the service of a luxury company. And she is increasingly shopping online rather than taking the time to visit a flagship store. Lisa likes the ease with which she can find products on the Internet, compared to spending all day looking for the most appealing items at the mall.

CLIMBER: KNOWS WHAT HE WANTS

Meet Frank. He is 40 years old, and he knows what things are worth. He wants good value for money, and in his world, luxury brands are just that. He has several years of experience as a business consultant and is on his way to becoming a partner at his company. His self-confidence has

Brand placement

Luxury success relies
on correctly positioning
a brand among the
four different types of
luxury consumer.

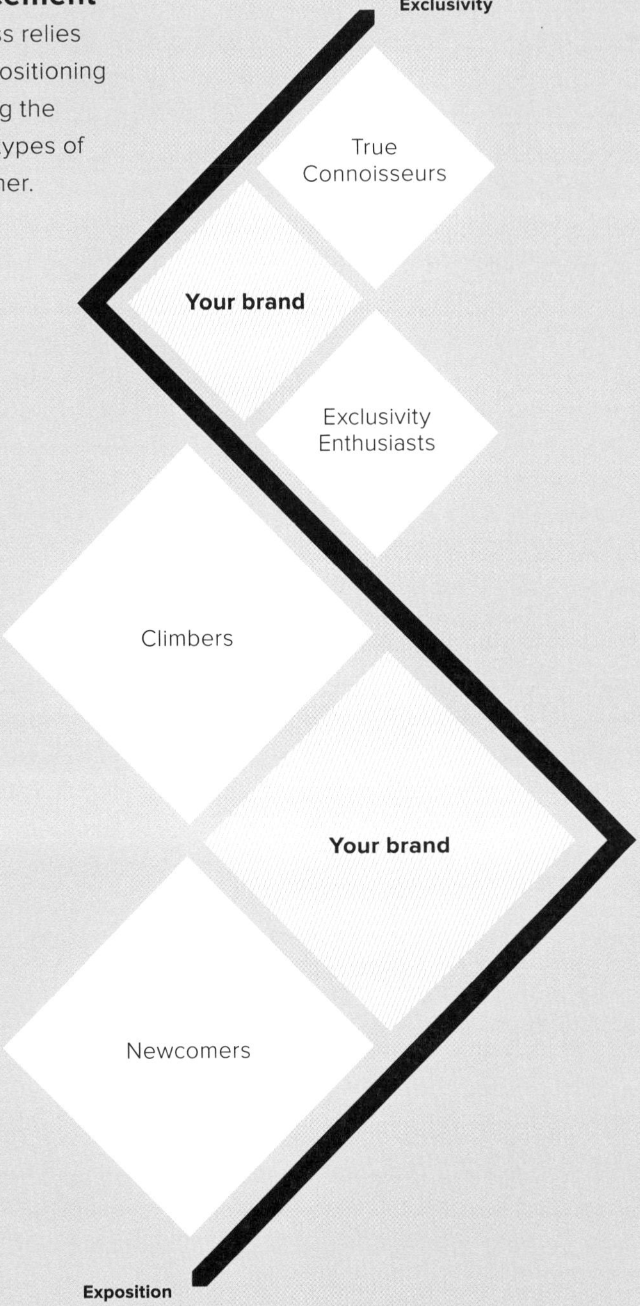

Exclusivity

True
Connoisseurs

Your brand

Exclusivity
Enthusiasts

Climbers

Your brand

Newcomers

Exposition

Source: Roland Berger Strategy Consultants

increased over the years. He knows what he wants and is willing to pay a premium for luxury products that fit and underline his personality. Since his salary is now considerably higher than a couple of years ago, he can easily afford high-quality luxury products. But buying the "brand" is not enough for Frank. He wants those products to be of outstanding quality and highly unique. It is no coincidence that he wears an older Rolex wristwatch with an acrylic crystal. Aficionados will know that this is a rare vintage timepiece, from a period before the company switched to sapphire crystals. For Frank, luxury purchases have become about more than just consumption, and he sees a vintage Rolex as a good investment. Although Frank enjoys reading magazines like *GQ*, celebrities in fashion spreads do not really influence his shopping choices. He is not going to change his favourite fashion label just because of what David Beckham is wearing in an advertisement. Classic celebrity marketing does not have great influence on the buying choices of this group of consumers. But guess what does? The Internet. The Climber is especially present in all kinds of social media networks and forums, and what his contacts say about a purchase or experience is critical to his buying behaviour.

EXCLUSIVITY ENTHUSIAST: ONLY THE BEST WILL DO

Meet Maria. She is 52 years old. Over the years, she has learned that less is more, but she still has very high standards. This means she is constantly looking to trade up, provided the market offers a good reason. For example, she wears an older gold watch by Patek Philippe but drives the newest 7-series BMW. If you visited Maria at her spacious yet tasteful apartment, you would see *Vogue* and similar high-fashion magazines on her coffee table. But, for her, luxury products are not an end in themselves. They are an opportunity to maintain standards in her uncluttered lifestyle. It is no surprise that she seeks brands that do not shout out "luxury". Still, those brands she does select often evoke nods of acknowledgment and appreciative looks from people she respects. Maria is also particular about where she spends time. She prefers the flair of luxury department stores to Internet shopping, even though she generally knows exactly what she wants. Still, the personal sales environment is an important aspect of trading up. She wants the feeling that she is not alone in her quest for quality, that other people understand her priorities and that they appreciate them. There have always been people who were prepared to have less, as long as what they had was the very best.

TRUE CONNOISSEUR: NUANCES, PLEASE

Meet Bernhard and Jessica. They are both over 60, and have nothing to prove to anyone. Anyone but themselves, that is. They have the homes, the cars and the yacht. At this stage, they are looking for subtleties, immaterial pleasures, nuanced experiences. The sparkle and bouquet of a particularly rare Champagne, the crystal waters and sweet tropical air of an exclusive resort in Tulum, Mexico – these might be the kinds of things sought after by True Connoisseurs. Bernhard has retired from his job as the CEO of a large corporation. What counts for this couple is that luxury fits their style. The latest fads in fashion are something they respond to with a raised eyebrow, if at all. Bernhard and Jessica certainly have their very own style, developed and shaped over the course of many decades of personal and professional experience. They do not feel the urge to impress anyone through their buying choices, and the popularity of a brand means little to them. For Bernhard and Jessica, quality, tradition and excellent service are of paramount importance. Price is no longer an object, as long as everything else fits. The couple makes choices based on the "inner qualities" of a prod-uct. The product needs to convey a classic elegance rather than sport brash and ostentatious features. They prefer fashion labels which are not widely known but have a high reputation in certain circles for quality and exclu-sivity, or tailor-made clothing. They are famously indifferent to opinion, or to the labels or products luxury consumers may be buying at any given moment. In fact, the couple prefers products from quality manufacturers with such a small output that only a few people have ever heard of them. Inconspicuous consumption is one of the sure signs of a True Connoisseur. There have always been True Connoisseurs. In the past, they were probably best known to gallerists and jewellers, and maybe high-end travel agents. But today such people have to compete with new attractions.

Continued on page 52

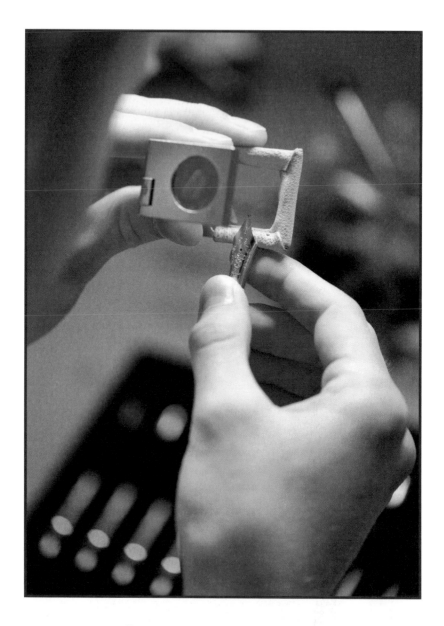

From pen company to luxury brand
Montblanc is now a luxury empire that leverages the legacy
of its pen to sell handbags, jewellery and perfume. The company has
created a tradition and legacy that almost transcends nationality.

OTHER MARKETS, SIMILAR CONSUMERS

We believe that gaining a knowledge of the four luxury target groups and their mindsets is a prerequisite for success in today's luxury market. Still, the way luxury target groups behave and how their decision-making unfolds is also influenced by external factors. Though globalisation is a key source of growth of the luxury products industry, in national markets there are some very specific factors taking shape and setting parameters. Consequently, we are faced with a customer base that is multifaceted, fragmented and liquid. To view actual consumer behaviour up close, we have selected examples from four countries, with differing proportions of luxury target groups and market characteristics: the United States, Russia, the United Arab Emirates and India.

UNITED STATES

One will come across all four types of consumers in the United States, with a certain tendency toward Exclusivity Enthusiasts. Most buyers of luxury items in America share a strong affection for brands. Among the affluent and wealthy population there is a widespread acceptance of showing one's success by buying luxury products. But in recent years, the people who buy luxury in America have changed quite a bit. Excellent quality and product design have become much more important. Many luxury consumers see the purchase of a well-designed, high-quality product as a "treat", while status, price and the exclusivity of a product have become less important.

This is partly due to the rise of a new class of affluent consumers who are better educated, wealthier, a lot more tech- and media-savvy and even more discerning consumers than other affluent Americans. They often recommend products to others, especially when it comes to electronic devices. They base most of their buying decisions on their personal style as well as on the "substance" and authenticity they associate with a company, instead of relying on the brand name alone. These "new affluents" are even more design-centric than other luxury consumers and would go out of their way to get the right item that aesthetically fits their lifestyle.

The demand for "experiential luxury" is also growing. Instead of buying cars and jewellery, many affluent customers have shifted their focus to helicopter snowboarding or learning to cook with a famous chef. Visible in the past, this trend towards experiential luxury has recently become more prominent. We will take a more in-depth look at it in chapter seven.

Another characteristic of the American market is its striking regionality. American luxury consumers focus mainly on the domestic market and typically do not travel abroad to buy exclusive products. This is thanks in part to the wide availability of luxury items in their home country, but also due to more attractive pricing compared to Europe.

RUSSIA

In Russia, most luxury consumers fall into the Newcomer and Climber categories. Conspicuous consumption still plays a large role here. Many luxury consumers in Russia prefer well-known labels that are easily recognised. Their main motivation is to gain status by buying a Ferrari, a Louis Vuitton bag or a Rolex watch. An increasing number of wealthy Russians are turning to domestic luxury brands such as Marussia Motors, a manufacturer of exclusive sports cars. The majority of Russian luxury consumers is not put off by high prices. On the contrary, the more expensive a luxury item is, the more coveted it becomes. Also, Russians are increasingly buying luxury in the fancy shopping districts of Moscow and St. Petersburg, where prices are often higher than in Western cities. Until recently, Russians flocked to luxury hotspots like New York, London or Paris. Purchasing an item with an enormous price tag distinguishes one from the rest. Despite the growing interest in domestic shopping, going abroad is still popular among Russians who aspire to be part of the international jet set. Russians are the world's second-largest group of tax-free shoppers, but big spenders driving big cars no longer dominate the Russian market like they once did. Luxury consumers in Russia are changing. The stereotypical opulence of the oligarchs is giving way to more subtle indulgences. A new generation of competitive, well-educated and affluent Russians aged 40–45, partly raised in Western countries, stands for a change in values. For this new generation of millonaires who did not take part in the mass privatisations during the early 1990s, a limited edition Bechstein piano or an exclusive work of art is a better way to show one's unique and refined taste than a diamond watch or a private jet. This new elite is leading the way to a new, more intellectual understanding of luxury.

UNITED ARAB EMIRATES

Each major city in the Emirates has its own distinct culture. But luxury consumers share a number of characteristics, whether they reside in Dubai, Sharjah or Abu Dhabi. International luxury brands are very popular among the well-to-do. Does the product have a large logo which will be recognised by many people? Then it's perfect for this market. Luxury consumers in the Emirates focus on accessories, especially on sunglasses. Sunglasses are experiencing a strong growth in sales here. That's perhaps not so unusual given the intensity of the sun and the prevalence of traditional costumes in everyday and business life. In cultures where dress is virtually uniform, the importance of sunglasses, writing instruments and other accessories increases. Those items offer some of the few opportunities Emiratis have to be unique and stand out. Having the right pen or the right shades is important. European luxury brands dominate the market here. American brands are much less popular. This is mainly due to the political and military role of the United States in the Middle East. The buying choices of Emiratis are also influenced by general trends in the luxury world, by the popular luxury fairs for ultra-high net worth individuals and by advertising that features Western celebrities. Emiratis are avid travellers and Western countries are their preferred destinations. Mutual trust, patience and the personal involvement of top-level sales executives are extremely important for members of the affluent elite who want to enlarge their collection of luxury items. And these qualities are also key to success in selling to them. It might well happen that the CEO of a company who wants to sell something to a reputable sheikh has to wait 48 hours until the sheikh eventually shows up – and then spends a million dollars in five minutes.

INDIA

Although an estimated 400 million people in India are living below the poverty line, the number of luxury consumers has grown. Dollar million-aires increased by 22 per cent from 2011 to 2012. Only Hong Kong had a higher growth rate of ultra-high net worth individuals during the same period. Newcomers, Climbers and Exclusivity Enthusiasts are the most important target groups in India. True Connoisseurship as described in the Continuum of Maturity can be found in the long-established, affluent families of India. For these families, high quality and craftsmanship are the main criteria used to assess the value of a luxury product. The traditional sari as an evening gown for women and items that combine traditional and modern styles are very popular.

Still, the luxury retail infrastructure in Indian cities is far less developed than in other important markets, such as in China. Major luxury shopping streets do not exist in India's big cities. Lavish mansions, yachts and expensive foreign cars are what India's wealthy elite is after. But branded goods? Not so much. As a result, the sales figures for Western luxury brands on the subcontinent are rather underwhelming. The few who do like to buy branded luxury goods do it while travelling to the world's luxury centres on private or business trips. Also, Indians do not like to splurge on most things. They are put off by price tags they deem too high, and they are famous for bargaining whenever they can. And since import taxes in India are notoriously high, it is often cheaper to pick up the phone and order something from a shop abroad and have it sent to you privately than to buy it in downtown Mumbai. Luxury shopping in India is still very much a personal matter. India is a one-to-one market. Direct enquir-ies or offers by CEOs or managers of luxury brands are tremendously important if companies want to sell high-priced items to India's affluent elite. Personal recommendations and word-of-mouth advertising from friends and acquaintances are essential if a product wants to appear on the radars of the rich. Here luxury shopping is an event for the whole family, a collective experience for sometimes up to 30 people.

"The new wealthy want their own luxury."

An interview with Jean-Claude Biver, chairman
of the board of Swiss watchmaker Hublot. The company
was founded in 1980 with a single model.

Hublot sells watches for €280,000, but recently began offering head-phones for €1,000. Are you serious?

We have to begin thinking outside the box in our industry. Why are we producing headphones now? Because they are a means of communication, like watches are. And the younger generation wears them as routinely as wristwatches used to be worn.

Don't traditional watch customers turn up their noses at that?

Not that I've noticed. Our sales in 2012 were 15 times what they were seven years earlier. The brand is currently doubling capacity at its produc-tion facilities in Geneva and is constructing an additional building. We're doing fine.

This sort of brand extension isn't causing any damage?

In all honesty, the headphones' function is rather good promotion. They aren't revenue drivers. These products, including our skis, high-tech sleds and carbon-fibre racing bicycles, demonstrate the distinctiveness of the brand. It wasn't an arbitrary decision. A special technology to improve the sound was built into the headphones, which we developed in cooperation with Monster. The racing bicycle was already equipped with an automatic gearing system in 2005. That was a sensation at the time, but today the technology is used on the Tour de France. We wanted to demonstrate Hublot's affinity with the future and technology.

Where do you see the potential of the Hublot brand?

When I joined Hublot in 2004, I wasn't primarily focused on the brand's potential, but on the potential of the customers. We are successful due to our customers, not our brand. The Ebel brand might have just as well been engraved on our watch faces. We would have been equally as successful as Hublot. What I'm trying to say is, that if we had been engaged somewhere else with the team we have at Hublot, we would be just as successful.

Where is the potential of your customers, then?

We have spoken to a new clientele. This is where the entire secret lies. We addressed new luxury. To get to know the new luxury of the 21st century, it would be best to head over to Soho House in Berlin. The people who go there have enough money to easily afford any other five-star hotel in Berlin. Why do they prefer to go to a hotel that, at least at first glance, looks as if its best days are behind it?

You have to explain a bit more, please.

The new wealthy want their own luxury, their own art, their own music. And not the look of their parents. The younger generation wants to express itself differently and have other luxury symbols than those of their fathers and grandfathers. Other luxury watch brands ignored younger buyers. They systematically addressed the normal, established luxury market. We were the only ones who spoke to the rappers, the football players and the basketball players.

Could you go into more specifics about the new luxury customer?

These are people who have so much confidence in themselves that they wear what they like and drive the car that they enjoy most. And not something that their social milieu dictates to them, as was customary for decades, even in the Western world. These are people who have enough strength and self-confidence to say, "I just don't care what other people think, I'm wearing that."

Why are we producing headphones now?
Because they are a means of communication, like watches.
And the younger generation wears them
as routinely as wristwatches used to be worn.

How many watches does the typical Hublot customer own?

Two, three on average. Our best customer, by the way, is a German who owns 150 Hublot watches.

Hublot belongs to LVMH. What has that brought with it?

The group assisted us in increasing name recognition in various countries. And then people said, "Oh, you're part of LVMH, that's great!" That means something around the world, and brings prestige. And then LVMH was extremely helpful in getting us store locations that nobody would ever have suggested otherwise. In 2009, no one would have thought to offer Hublot the prime address on Place Vendôme in Paris when it became available.

How important is a retail shop in the Internet era?

At the moment we have 55 shops. We are adding more. In the course of the next three years we want to be offering Hublot watches exclusively at 120 boutiques around the world.

And all those shops with the Internet-savvy customers of today?

Of course that's a contradiction. But a watch is like a pair of shoes. You have to try them on. And I can only advise anyone to not buy a pair of shoes on the Internet. The same holds true for watches. Even if you are able to buy them on the Internet, you should place it on your wrist at least once. Along with the diameter, other dimensions such as height, the width of the band and the watch's weight also contribute to the wearing comfort.

A watch is like a pair of shoes. You have to try them on.
And I can only advise anyone to not buy a pair
of shoes on the Internet. The same holds true for watches.
You should place it on your wrist at least once.

What is your biggest challenge in reaching customers?

This comes down to retail shops themselves. They are by far the most important and best instruments of communication. Each boutique sells about 20 to 30 watches every month, so that's about 1,500 sold watches in total for us around the world. The majority of people who enter our shops leave with a watch.

You hold the record for selling the most expensive watch in the world, at €5 million. And you have a current model available for €1 million. What type of customer purchases something like that?

You cannot describe customers in this price range. But you really do find them everywhere. For instance, we sold three of the €1-million watches to Germans. But we also had a customer from Las Vegas and one from Istanbul. First off, these customers spend €1 million the way you and me might spend €1,000. For €1,000, you might buy an Omega, a Tag Heuer or a Longines. So it's all relative. Second, these are people who know that a watch could actually be worth that much. Many people wouldn't even begin to understand, and say, "How can that be? It's a scam!" So these customers need expertise and knowledge, in things like the timekeeping mechanism, the gemstones or other materials. They must be able to recognise the substantive value.

How has luxury marketing changed for the various customer segments?

Back in the 1970s, the majority of watch companies didn't undertake any sort of marketing. The product did the marketing, and that was it. The credo was to produce the world's most precise watch. And then came the quartz watches. Companies spoke more about the technology than they did about emotions. The paradigm change came through fashion.

The new wealthy want their own luxury,
their own art, their music.
And not the look of their parents.

What do you mean?

The fashion industry discovered us. In a 1970 issue of *Vogue* you won't see watches anywhere. No editorial. No advertisements. And now? You find something every couple of pages. At least 10 watch ads in every magazine nowadays. No one buys a mechanical watch today just because it is particularly precise.

Speaking of fashion, does Hublot do any market research to see which colours to use next year?

We never conduct market research. What can market research do for such a niche product? We would never be able to achieve a large enough representative sample. Our customers spend an average of €15,000 for a watch. That's what makes luxury marketing so difficult.

So how do you come up with things like leopard prints on the wristbands?

It's pure instinct. We just know our customers' fashion tastes and wishes in detail. If bikinis for 2014 are violet or blue, we adjust immediately by having the same bands or watch casings. There's no excuse if your watch does not match your Hermès handbag, for instance. Furthermore, we're simply very open to new things. We don't limit ourselves to tradition alone. We constantly remain on the lookout and keep our ears to the ground. We always say "yes" to new things. Then later on we consider whether or not it should become a "no".

Which markets are most important for Hublot?

In absolute numbers, we sell the most watches in the United States. But we have by far the highest market share in Japan. Next comes Singapore. After that, the most important markets are Mexico, Brazil and Russia.

How do you serve the interests of the different markets?

Internationally there's a learning curve. Think of children who would like to play a musical instrument. First, they learn acoustic guitar before daring to try the electric. To understand the future you need the past. Markets function exactly the same way. In China, for instance, they are absolutely interested in the past. In mechanics, tradition. Sports are uninteresting for the luxury segment there. Russians, on the other hand, buy something that is focused on the future rather than the past. In the emerging markets, a visible brand image plays a large role, while other countries still require tradition. But you cannot head towards the future without the past. Just like jumping. You need one foot on the ground in order to leap far ahead.

What does this mean for the product portfolio? Doesn't it inevitably lead to too many models and a dilution of the brand image?

Our product range is indeed quite broad. We release about 100 new models per year. However, the trick is that they are for the most part limited editions. By next year, 80 per cent of the models will no longer be available. Still, we earn 70 per cent of our revenue with 120 basic models. The limited editions are offered exclusively in the boutiques, which attracts customers.

Could you sum up Hublot's recipe for success?

Ultimately, a brand's substance is the most important thing. It must maintain a substantial balance between marketing and true innovation. Research delivers the authenticity. When you strongly advertise the brand, as we do, you have to deliver substance through research and development all the more. Marketing always seems to pull energy from a product. You must counter this through committed research and development and reach a balance.

Ultimately, a brand's substance is the most important thing. It must maintain a substantial balance between marketing and true innovation. Research delivers the authenticity.

So you invest just as much in research as you do in marketing?

Due to our sponsorship of the 2014 Football World Cup in Brazil, this is impossible at the moment. But over a time frame of 10 years these expenditures shouldn't differ by more than 5 per cent. Otherwise you're selling a fashion product.

CHAPTER THREE

EAST IS THE NEW WEST

Adapting a Eurocentric
luxury market to Asian dynamics
and demands

RETHINKING LUXURY

She is not just China's first high-profile first lady. A professional singer, Peng Liyuan is collecting an impressive number of firsts that go beyond her public role and illustrate the newfound confidence of the Asian powerhouse. Peng began making headlines abroad as she accompanied her husband, Chinese president Xi Jinping, on his first state trips abroad. What observers noticed as she stepped off the plane was that she was clothed entirely by high-end Chinese designers. Where the country's elite had previously looked westward for inspiration, Peng announced the arrival of Chinese designers on the international luxury market.

The ascension of China as both a buying and selling power was a trend France's Hermès decided to embrace in 2008 by launching a new luxury brand for the Chinese market. The brand would be produced by Chinese designers, aimed at Chinese luxury buyers and would have production based in China. Although the trend was clear in 2008, no one expected the Chinese market and its consumers to become such an important component of the global luxury market as quickly as it did. In 2012, the Chinese luxury market became the biggest in Asia, surpassing Japan, and the second largest in the world. Wealthy Chinese from Greater China (including Macau, Hong Kong and Taiwan) spent an estimated €27 billion on luxury items in that year, about 12 per cent of the total €212-billion market. The country is home only to about one-third of the Asian population, but it mints thousands of millionaires a year and its super-rich are steadily increasing in number. This creation of new money is driving the demand for luxury products among the Chinese, and the emergence of a new shopping class already has broad implications for the market. As noted in our opening chapter, the traditional logic in luxury is that the market is immune to swings in both taste and economies. Luxury, the logic goes, sets the agenda. Buyers follow. But that logic may now be outdated. The next Asian – or even Chinese – generation may have completely different tastes and demands than previous generations. There are already signs that they have different desires, and Hermès' move seems to acknowledge that paradigm shift.

Hermès launched its new brand with a single store in Shanghai. The interior is covered in hexagonal white fabric that adds a soft, bright texture to the walls and highlights the store's light, wood-grain furniture. The furnishings have no sharp edges and are often curved. The brand, Shang Xia, was created from the ground up by Shanghai designer Jiang Qiong Er and means "up-down" in Mandarin, an obvious reference to yin and yang. Designer Jiang has said she wants to recast old crafts in a new light to ensure subsequent generations appreciate the products. "I believe that the rise of the Chinese economy will foster craftsmanship and design, but it will take some patience," Jiang says. "We believe this may become a crucial component in responding to global demographic changes and an economic shift in the luxury market: adapting to once-foreign Asian tastes and cultures as Asian consumers gain self-confidence and become comfortable in their role as trendsetters."

SLEEPING DRAGON

Yet the future of the luxury market is Asian, whether it is selling products in the eastern continent or catering to Asian shoppers in markets such as the United States and Europe. In the past, Europe, with its centuries-old traditions, was always king. But that was yesterday's world. Once-silent populations that are gaining a voice, combined with new flows of money, means luxury consumers are becoming more Asian, with cultural and familial roots often alien to traditional European makers of luxury products and services. Luxury consumers have traditionally longed for purchases that are steeped in European craftsmanship, but we believe that is changing. For now, Asian buyers are still sticking to traditional European luxury, but there is plenty of room for new brands or even the emergence of unexpected tastes – Korea's ascension as a cultural bastion is one such surprise. For us, East is the new West.

When we talk about the East, in large part we are talking about China. The country's rise from a sizeable and boisterous outpost of communism to a capitalist bulwark has created a gold rush for the luxury industry. The country took over the pole position much faster than even experts predicted. In 2005, Japan was still the Asian luxury leader and affluent Chinese were only spending one-tenth as much as their Japanese peers. Just seven years later, the Chinese began pulling away from Japanese luxury consumers. China's turbo growth has sparked a rocket-propelled expansion of luxury spending. Although China lags Germany in the number of total high net worth individuals, it has more mid- and ultra-high net worth individuals, illustrating the country's swift ascension. It's not just dominating because it is the biggest fighter in the ring. China's well-heeled consumers are unique. The reason is basic: the government still keeps a tight grip on free speech, but allows its citizens to spend the money flowing into the country nearly unfettered. This translates to consumers who are eager to express themselves through purchases, since they are allowed few other forms of expression. The Chinese are transitioning into a mature market and are moving away from the conspicuous consumption segment of luxury buying, putting them on the lookout for sophisticated brands. More detailed information on the size of Asia's luxury markets is shown on the infographic on page 70, and we take a look at the leading position China's consumers have taken in the infographic on page 73.

We believe the studies show the Chinese are outpacing everyone in the world when it comes to how highly they value luxury. Affluent Chinese shoppers assign much more meaning to luxury purchases than their counterparts in the West. It is almost as if they are asserting a new identity, and money is the empowering factor. China's luxury shoppers are also younger than their counterparts in the West. We discovered that about 45 per cent of the country's luxury spending comes from people under 35, compared with 28 per cent in Western Europe.

A NEW INDUSTRIAL REVOLUTION

It is no secret that younger shoppers are more willing to part with their wealth than older, more conservative consumers. Age distribution is not the only differentiating factor for Chinese consumers. Luxury has become so important to the country's nouveau riche that high-end spending has seeped down to income groups that can barely afford it. We also found that households with annual incomes equivalent to just under $40,000 are regularly buying luxury products. And, above them, upper-middle-class households now make up about 12 per cent of the country's luxury purchases. The country is going through a huge transformation. "What they're going through from the consumption perspective is like what we went through in the Industrial Revolution," says Brian Buchwald, CEO of the Bomoda media venture targeting affluent Chinese fashion consumers.

Since Chinese consumers are so aware of what those around them are aware of, non-traditional luxury brands have a challenging time. Chinese consumers prefer to buy brands others are talking about – or have told them about. The top three luxury fashion brands for the Chinese are Chanel, Louis Vuitton and Gucci. The Chinese are also very cautious shoppers. This is why having a strong presence in the country is vital. Local stores or events allow hesitant buyers the opportunity to see and feel potential purchases before taking an exclusive item home. Initial purchases of a specific brand are almost always done in China, but shopping abroad is also on the increase. Luxury brands are already doing an excellent job of responding. Heavyweights such as Gucci and Hermès have expanded

China is a growing force in luxury consumption

The luxury market in Greater China, including Macau, Hong Kong and Taiwan, has already surpassed Japan.

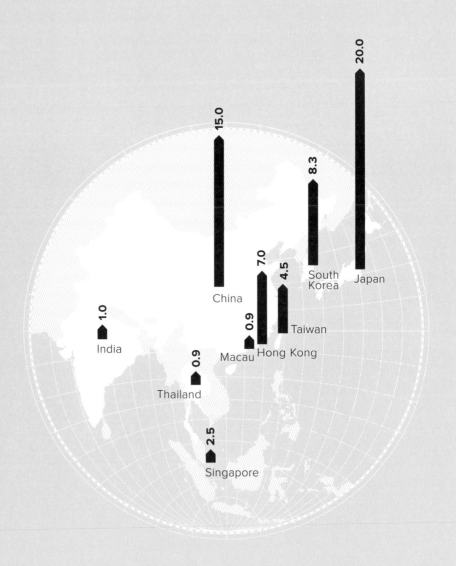

Asian luxury goods market, figures from 2012, estimate in billions of euros

Source: Altagamma Foundation, Worldwide Luxury Markets Monitor, 2013

their networks of Chinese stores into the double digits, having had just a handful in the past. We address the importance of bricks-and-mortar retail for luxury in chapter six.

Once away from home, Chinese shoppers are more prone to acquisitions, with good reason. High customs duties raise the price of luxury goods at domestic stores. When looking at China, companies should assume that customs charges will add about 30 per cent to the cost of goods there – but a number of factors can actually boost that disparity to as much as 70 per cent. For small accessories and incidentals, those fees do not mean much to the rich. However, when that fee is added to the bill for a leather coat, watch or car, it can put it out of reach or desirability. Chinese consumers know that opting to buy elsewhere can even pay for itself. They would often rather spend that 30 per cent on an airfare and a hotel in Paris. The Chinese Ministry of Commerce knows that customs duties are scaring away consumers, and several years ago debated drastic reductions. However, officials worried that changing the fees could be seen as favouring the rich, leading to inaction. Although the government cut tariffs on some imports, such as powdered milk in 2012, it's still collecting high fees on luxury items.

The high cost of shopping at home has created some differences in where the country's luxury shoppers spend their money. The majority of them still shop in mainland China, despite the tariffs. Only a small minority entirely eschews the domestic market. However, about half of Chinese luxury customers shop abroad and at home. This makes them a powerful force. Most of this "shopping abroad" still takes place in Hong Kong and Macau, but Europe is a shopping destination that is on the radar of a rapidly increasing number of Chinese luxury customers.

CHINESE LUXURY IS GLOBAL LUXURY

Although technically the Chinese still spend most of their luxury cash within China, interest is continually growing in shopping in Europe as well as in the United States, which remains the world's number one luxury market. Tourist shoppers are a demographic that should not be ignored when trying to attract consumer attention in Europe. Why? Some analysts believe Italy's Prada got half of its European sales (excluding Italy) from Chinese tourists in 2012. That buying boost helped increase the fashion house's 2012 European sales by one-third. Luxury companies must also consider nearby Asian markets to lure in Chinese shoppers. Places such as Singapore and South Korea have special sway among affluent Chinese consumers.

Consider the popularity of the song *Gangnam Style* and its accompanying video – many young Chinese consider Psy and his K-Pop ilk much hipper than their once-dominant Japanese counterparts. Indeed, part of what is attractive to young people has always been finding trends from somewhere previously ignored by their parents. The intrusion of South Korean culture into China has meant a blessing for the South Korean tourist industry, with the number of visits growing strongly each year. That is partly the result of expanding wealth but must also be related to Chinese interest in South Korean culture.

Greater China – including Macau, Hong Kong and Taiwan – is a vital market for foreign luxury companies. While traditional luxury brands have succeeded by simply showing up with retail stores and heavy online presences, many, like Hermès, are trying unique approaches to skim the buoyant Chinese market even more. Hermès' rival Kering has taken an even more direct approach to expansion in the Chinese market: buying customers. In late 2012, the company acquired a majority of local jeweller Qeelin. It did not say how much it paid but maintains the company is profitable and well-positioned with 14 stores in China. Its jewellery goes for between HK$20,000 (€2,000) and HK$300,000 (€30,000) and is even available in Europe and Japan. In our opinion, acquisitions can be an excellent means of getting into China. Local brands such as watchmakers Shanghai Watch or Seagull have yet to realise their full potential and can benefit from the unique perspective and expertise of a larger company.

The unbridled growth of the Chinese luxury market has not gone unnoticed by the Chinese Communist Party. After a leadership change in 2012, the party cracked down on spending by government officials, leading to a drop in spending, both on luxury gifts and on services for administrators used to a

Luxury consumers are becoming increasingly Asian

Chinese consumers now make up one-quarter of all the luxury customers in the world. Almost one-quarter of luxury consumers are European.

1995

31%
European

31%
Japanese

27%
American

7%
other Asian

3%
RoW*

1%
Chinese

2012

25%
Chinese

24%
European

20%
American

14%
Japanese

11%
other Asian

6%
RoW*

* Rest of the world

Source: Altagamma Foundation Luxury Goods Worldwide Market Study, 2012

lavish, state-sponsored lifestyle. While the anti-corruption and anti-conspicuous consumption campaign had a direct effect on luxury revenue, there were hints that the party might in the future do more to influence the luxury sector.

Officials have said they are concerned about the rift between the country's rich and poor (or even super-rich and super-poor) and, in February 2013, banned advertisements of ostentatious goods and services on the country's state television and radio stations. The ads, it said, "publicised incorrect values and helped create a bad social ethos." Since this is the second time in two years the party has imposed such a prohibition, the direction the country's leadership is taking should not be ignored. Companies should consider both the party's moves against luxury brands and the previously mentioned moves to reconsider tolls because they are a sort of yin and yang. While there is political concern about the rift between the rich and the poor, the party has also made changes that favour commerce.

FROM ONLY CHILD TO STEPCHILD: JAPAN

After being on the centre stage of the global luxury segment for decades, Japan and Japanese buyers have fallen from the limelight in just a matter of years. The Japanese luxury market has a great history. It began blossoming in the 1970s as the rich went abroad and brought home hand-made treasures exuding quality and tradition. However, the exuberance that once made the country an emerging luxury market has now created a saturated one. Worse yet, like Japanese wealth, that market is deteriorating. Currently the world's third largest economy, Japan may slip to fourth by 2050, according to predictions by HSBC. While China is on an upswing, Japan appears to be at least stalling. However, even though the country has just a fraction of the population of China, it still has plenty of money, and money being spent. The spotlight may no longer be on the country, but the Japanese luxury market is only slightly behind China.

Luxury brands have not – and should not – give up on Japan. Burberry, along with Prada and Hermès, has twice as many stores in Japan as it does in, for example, the United States. Japanese customers account for about

13 per cent of Louis Vuitton fashion and leather goods sales, and 40 per cent of well-heeled Japanese own a Vuitton product. The Japanese market is also at the most advanced of the four basic stages of luxury evolution. It is in the final, meaningful stage that is defined by shoppers who live within and are comfortable navigating the luxury lifestyle and markets. Luxury products in Japan are part of daily life. In Japan, there is no more discovery or exuberance. Affluent Japanese consumers have been spending big on products and services for as long as they remember and they know what they like – and what they do not like. In this stage, there is very little room for convincing a buyer to try something new or different. To be sure, consumers at this stage still spend on luxury – and they spend plenty – but they are the ones in the driver's seat, deciding on which direction they want to take.

Satisfied that they know what they are buying and what they want, Japanese, like many modern luxury shoppers, are now more concerned with the experience of shopping – or buying experiences in the form of services. This perhaps explains the high numbers of retail stores in Japan and the sheer size of its market. Retail can create a unique experience for consumers buying shoes, watches or even cars. Mere spending is not enough of a thrill anymore. Now a V-12 car has to be delivered at a race track and a haute couture dress should come directly from the designer's atelier after the buyer sits front row at a fashion show – all expenses covered by the brand. We talk more about the importance of delivering an experience in chapter seven. Many brands have already embraced these consumers. Gucci built not just a flagship store, but a flagship building in Ginza that features a cinema for restored Italian classics. Cosmetics company Shiseido created the Shiseido Parlour, with an art gallery, restaurant and tea room. Other brands opt for special VIP sales or one-off events for loyal customers to emphasise an air of exclusivity, or create a sense that buyers are brand insiders helping to guide the trend. However, the move to offer more in Japan has not always paid off. Versace abandoned the market in 2009 after an expansion failed, but it's back now.

Then there is the evolution of Japanese consumers themselves. The next generation is very different than their predecessors, in part because of the confidence created by generations of wealth. Where their parents demanded

Continued on page 78

Gucci Ginza Café
Gucci's flagship store in Tokyo's Ginza District is much more
than just a shop: the integrated brand experience includes a gallery and
a Gucci café which serves cake branded with the company's logo.

proven quality, robust materials and a history of craftsmanship, Japan's modern luxury consumers are not afraid to mix and match between high-end products and their more mainstream, lower-cost brethren. If rich Japanese people are more concerned with what they think of a product than how they are perceived while using it, then it is likely that they would pass that sense, at least partially, on to their children. Today in Japan, being an informed buyer is knowing what is worth spending money on and where frugality highlights your buying intelligence. Rich young Japanese shoppers mix trips to Lamborghini, Prada and Hermès with stops at Uniqlo and luxury outlets.

We see brand diversification as a good example of how to react to a saturated luxury market. Confident in its position at the top of the luxury ladder in Japan, Burberry created Japan-only brands to appeal even more to fickle youth with less money in their pockets than their parents. Burberry Black Label and Blue Label offer clothes and accessories at a discount to their parent brand – as much as 90 per cent on some items, such as handbags. In the eyes of some, these items then no longer qualify as luxury, but if the products can be produced at a significant discount without compromising quality, it is money Burberry would not otherwise be getting from the selective buyers. Arguments can be made about diluting brands and images. However, it is a trick Lanvin is also trying with Lanvin en Bleu and Lanvin Collection. These two Japan-only brands are positioned lower and cheaper, hoping to keep some of the money away from Uniqlo. Nor does this stop at individual brands. Outlet malls are a common sight in Japan, with 39 throughout the country and the biggest debuting in 2012, near Tokyo in Kisarazu. Who is there? The list of who is not may be shorter.

THE BROADBAND SUPERPOWER: SOUTH KOREA

Another Asian luxury market we note is South Korea, which has posted strong growth for nearly a decade, though its market remains about one-third the size of Greater China's. The country's blossoming cultural influence is the first reason to pay attention to South Korea. The country has not just made it onto the radar of China's wealthy, it has made it onto the radar of almost everyone. Sure, that is in part thanks to the fascinating pop star Psy. But it is also because the country's mass-market consumer items are household names alongside other Asian competitors. Brands such as Samsung, LG and Hyundai have piqued the curiosity of international consumers. Even tourism is booming. South Korea is equally famous for its upmarket luxury multi-label stores, where shoppers find suits by Armani, shoes by Salvatore Ferragamo and Gucci sunglasses in one large store or mall. Luxury Hall West and Luxury Hall East, both located in Seoul's affluent Apgujeong-dong district, are the most notable examples for this popular concept.

South Korea is also enjoying an economic renaissance, with ambitious companies hoping to secure its position as an electronics powerhouse. The country is also attractive to luxury marketers because of its willingness to embrace the Internet. Luxury companies can reach Korean consumers without leaving home by establishing a Korean web presence that remains true to their brand image and level of opulence. And Koreans love luxury. One reason is because they want to reward themselves for working exceptionally long hours – about 5 per cent of an affluent consumer's budget is spent on luxury items, one percentage point higher than their Japanese peers. "There is a remarkable focus on supplying branded, individualistic clothing products, rather than the ultra-cheap basics you might expect from their equivalents in the West. Koreans shop online at eBay's Gmarket for basics and go to the stores for their bling," says Christian Oliver, a *Financial Times* columnist in Seoul.

Asia and Asian consumers are the new look of luxury. Their pocketbooks and cultures will shape the future of affluent buying. Their tastes currently mirror the traditional tastes and brands of luxury. After all, luxury is steeped in history. It is a way to buy into a past that was more careful and potentially more exclusive. Asia may be changing that. The emergence of China as a super shopping power must mean change – it is a different culture with a different background and an odd political structure that allows capitalism within communism. We aren't just saying East is the new West because it has a nice ring to it.

HOW TO...
Four strategies for successful
e-commerce in China

It seems obvious that the world's most rapidly growing market for luxury products would also be an ideal playing field for e-commerce. However, as some overly enthusiastic entrepreneurs have discovered, it is just as easy to miscalculate the needs of this powerful new audience. Here are four pointers to help companies make it over the finish line.

1. Foster relationships with brands

As we have established in this chapter, Chinese customers largely prefer European-made luxury goods with a long history of excellence and are intensely loyal to their favourite brands. By that token, they will also be more likely to give credit to brands that have made their reputation in the West. In fact, trust is one of the deciding factors in making online purchases. Or rather, distrust. Research into the buying habits of luxury consumers has shown that while close to two-fifths of these shoppers in China already use the Internet to gain information about products, only 8 per cent of them go online to spend money. That reluctance is rooted in the fact that China is still thought of as a hotbed for fakes – even by the Chinese. Paying for a luxury item online, only to receive a counterfeited product in the mail, has discouraged people from making purchases.

2. Make service a priority

Getting the product to the customer quickly and, better yet, free of charge, is a good start. But the service should not end there. Apply the same rigour to after-delivery care. Thecorner.cn has a call centre to deal with anything from availability of product to returns. Additionally, a sound and easy-to-navigate payment process is vital for catering to customers' convenience. In the grand scheme of things, it might not seem like a big deal for a company to implement these structures, but it can make a huge difference in determining their success. It is also vital to present a website in Chinese that matches Chinese tastes. Customers there expect websites to be flashy and complex – almost gaudy by Western standards. The small details make the difference.

3. Start now

It was only in 2010 that Emporio Armani opened for e-commerce in China, the first Western fashion brand to do so, with a small band of others following suit and companies exploring options for multi-brand e-commerce. But since then the number of people who make at least one luxury purchase per year has quadrupled, and total luxury spending has gone up 50 per cent. Investors are picking up on this shifting attitude. In February 2013, a consortium led by Saudi prince Alwaleed bin Talal invested $400 million in homegrown Chinese startup 360buy.com. The advantage for first-movers that overcomes their hesitation at putting up the money lies not just in gaining ground on competitors, but in having time to work on and perfect the business model, making it run smoothly before the rest of the field can catch up. Because here is another number: the Chinese online market is projected to grow by more than six times by 2015.

4. Use local social media networks

Social media is more important in China than in most other markets. The country often operates according to "guanxi", a Chinese word for personal network. The Chinese rely on their own personal network to make buying decisions, and value highly the opinions of those closest to them. Since social networks can be seen as a digital extension of guanxi, they should be an integral part of every marketing project. Forget the usual suspects here, as the country has its own social networks, which vary depending on age. The largest – and youngest – is Qzone, a favourite among older children and teens. RenRen appeals to those in their twenties, while Sina Weibo reaches people firmly in their careers. Marketers should focus on the social media site that fits them best – and do everything in Chinese.

"We're not conquering, we're offering."

An interview with Jiang Qiong Er,
CEO of Shang Xia, the Chinese luxury brand of Hermès,
which now also has a Paris boutique.

Shang Xia is considered to be China's first domestic luxury brand. Why aren't there many others?

Shang Xia is walking on a new path. We actually don't position ourselves as a luxury brand, even though people often say that we are. Shang Xia is a brand of 21st-century fine living, where contemporary design meets Chinese heritage crafts. It's new and it will need quite a long time to develop. We hope there will be more companions walking the same path as we are. That way our Chinese inheritance could be continued in a healthy and substantial way.

How did it all start?

I was introduced to traditional Chinese art when I was little, and had the opportunity to explore it in different fields of art. As I understood more and more about Chinese craftsmanship and the deft skills of craftsmen over the years, I was truly touched by the power and beauty of their work. Over time, I developed a dream to share this appreciation with the world. In 2006, I told Patrick Thomas, CEO of Hermès, and Pierre-Alexis Dumas, artistic director of Hermès, about my vision and we decided to create this new baby called Shang Xia. It took us a few years to build the team, searching for the finest craftsmen throughout China, and interpret it with contemporary design. In 2009 Shang Xia was officially founded in Shanghai, with its first worldwide boutique opening in Beijing in September 2010.

Right now most Chinese luxury customers seem to be interested in European brands, products and heritage. Will they start embracing their own tradition more?

We definitely see more and more Chinese customers at Shang Xia. As a matter of fact, our Beijing boutique caters to up to 70 per cent Chinese customers, embracing their heritage and culture. I believe that emotion is the key to one's art of living. The finest touch of craftsmanship, innovative design and contemporary lifestyle are all linked by a personal touch. Without a true emotional understanding this link is disconnected. The

*I believe that emotion is the key to one's
art of living. The finest touch of craftsmanship,
innovative design and contemporary
lifestyle are all linked by a personal touch.*

inheritance of our culture and fine art will lead Chinese customers to come along the way with us as they're searching to fulfil their emotional demands.

Could the tables even be turned soon and Chinese and other Asian luxury brands start conquering Europe?

I wouldn't use the word "conquer". I would call it an offering. The Western world has a long history of appreciating culture and art from the East. So the revival of contemporary Chinese craftsmanship and design will also be shared and appreciated by international citizens, without doubt. The question is not about turning tables. The question is about time. Unfortunately, in the past 100 years China has faded from the cultural continuum. I believe that the rise of the Chinese economy will foster craftsmanship and design, but it will take some patience. When we opened our first overseas boutique in Paris in September 2013, we didn't want to do it big, but we wanted to do it well.

Should more European luxury brands form collaborations such as the one between you and Hermès? If so, what's the secret to a successful one?

I can only share what Shang Xia is keen to achieve. We are not another branch of Hermès, but we share the same value of pursuing the best quality. And we produce almost all of our objects in China, such as finely wrought homewares and elegant clothes, including sculptural dresses made from hand-felted cashmere in a centuries-old process with its typical attention to detail.

Continued on page 88

Flagship Bejing boutique
Shang Xia works to create
a modern Chinese aesthetic in both
its products and its stores.

Local craftsmen
The company employs native artisans
to create superlative products based on Chinese
traditions but using fresh designs.

*Nowadays, more people want something different.
In the first 30 years of economic
development, the Chinese did not have the
opportunity to pursue these desires.*

The Chinese luxury market comes with its own unique challenges. Many are concerned about the rift between the country's rich and poor. Are you seeing a political or cultural backlash against luxury spending, especially for Western brands?

For a while, Western luxury brands have been making inroads with the most fashion forward of the country's sizable population that has an appetite for luxury. However, the perception is slowly changing as many homegrown, high-end brands are being developed, often with a traditional bent and sophisticated designs. People used to desire anything from a luxury brand. Nowadays, more people want something different. In the first 30 years of economic development, the Chinese did not have the opportunity to pursue this desire. It was about fulfilling basic needs, not going hungry, not being cold. Now, we've started to return to our cultural roots. In the last five years, people have started to realise the importance of creativity and quality in China.

CHAPTER FOUR

IS BLING NO LONGER KING?

Logo luxury versus the rise of new values
that are dividing the market

RETHINKING LUXURY

"The era of the jet set is over."
It is a surprising statement coming
from a man who represents
one of the world's most venerated
luxury brands. Patrick-Louis Vuitton,
the great-great-grandson of
Louis Vuitton, has been director of
special orders for his family's company
for over 40 years, and oversees
the manufacturing of bespoke luggage.
His name is synonymous with prestige;
his services are some of the best
that money can buy. When customers
are looking for something even
more extravagant than the brand's
regular top-shelf products,
Monsieur Vuitton is the man they call.

So what prompted Vuitton to make his daring statement about the jet set? It would seem to be an affront to his clientele. "There will always be people who want to travel elegantly," he attests. "But business travellers are playing an increasingly bigger role. Among the customers who order bespoke luggage are people who travel 200 to 300 days out of the year." In other words, his customers are changing. Before, they would spend money on gimmicky indulgences. Over the years, Patrick-Louis Vuitton has produced trunks to transport everything from Barbie dolls to crystal champagne glasses. Nowadays, his clients are investing in luggage that will not just look impressive, but also serve a practical purpose.

Vuitton receives around 400 special orders a year, and is at the centre of the luxury market. Any change first felt by his company is likely to spread across the rest of the industry. In fact, we believe that the world of luxury has experienced a seismic shift in consumer behaviour. This is evidenced by an appreciation of values beyond a product's monetary worth. Consumers in mature markets are moving away from ostentatious displays of wealth towards a more understated form of spending. Examples are the popularity of brands like Bottega Veneta and Loro Piana, which famously do not have logos. Yet, they still let the consumer communicate something valuable: the appearance of cultured consumption. And although this change in attitude is most evident in established Western economies, it is becoming true for Asian consumers as well. Addressing it will be vital to the success of any luxury brand.

MOOD CHANGE

Less bling, more discretion. That was the message received by the elites from the financial crisis of 2008. When Wall Street collapsed, the self-proclaimed "Masters of the Universe" came down with it. These were bankers with almost unfathomable wealth, who surrounded themselves with status symbols to demonstrate their power. Men like the former Merrill Lynch CEO John Thain, who spent $1.2 million on remodelling an office. Or the executives of Citigroup, who thought it prudent to add another $50-million jet to their existing fleet, even as the bank was being bailed out by the US government. It seemed crass, greedy and out of touch with reality. And although the spending of the wealthy soon recovered to levels that preceded the crisis, a more sombre mood had replaced the frantic spending of the 1990s and early 2000s. Showing off was no longer seen as appropriate, either personally or socially.

DEVELOPING TASTES

Luxury purchases are emotional buys that have intangible values beyond their price. One result of the recession is that consumers want to express understatement, sophistication and thoughtfulness. For some of the most popular luxury brands, this development poses an interesting challenge. Companies have traditionally taken it for granted that they could sell customers anything, as long as it had an impressive name, a recognisable logo or was simply very, very expensive. Handbags, sports cars, watches – the bigger and shinier, the better. This habit of "conspicuous consumption" was first described by Thorstein Veblen in *The Theory of the Leisure Class* in 1899, in which the author argued that the rich use the accumulation of possessions to demonstrate their status in society. Veblen wrote, "The motive is emulation – the stimulus of an invidious comparison which prompts us to outdo those with whom we are in the habit of classing ourselves." According to Veblen, consumption is viewed as a competition in which products are used to gain advantage in distinguishing oneself from one's peers. However, what this theory does not take into account is that, as a person's wealth grows and becomes more established, their tastes develop along with it. We have identified four stages of consumption that companies should consider as they are reaching out to clients.

Stage 1: Ostentation

This mirrors what Veblen described in *The Theory of the Leisure Class*. When wealth is first accumulated, the consumer likes to demonstrate financial prowess by buying and displaying symbols of their status.

Stage 2: Differentiation

As consumers become accustomed to their status, they develop a sense of awareness. This helps them make more informed choices and demand more quality and elegance.

Stage 3: Knowledgeability

A class of informed consumers who see themselves more as collectors. They distinguish between products as they live out their personal passions and seek pleasure.

Stage 4: Meaningfulness

In this final stage, consumers demand products that will bring personal fulfilment, engage them in immaterial ways and satisfy a sense of experience.

Of these four stages, the last one offers an opportunity for luxury brands to bind customers in the long term. Instead of aiming for the throwaway success of a quickly sold lifestyle product, this could be a goal to consider. But how do you best engage customers' longing for refinement while providing them with an opportunity to demonstrate their expertise? David Brooks has some answers. In his 2000 book, *Bobos in Paradise*, *The New York Times* columnist first identified an emerging class of spenders, a composite of "bohemian" and "bourgeois". Brooks writes, "A new set of codes organises the consumption patterns of the educated class, encouraging some kinds of spending, which are deemed virtuous, and discouraging others that seem vulgar or elitist." Furthermore, "The members of the educated-class elite feel free to invest huge amounts of capital in things that are categorised as needs, but it is not acceptable to spend on mere wants […] A person who follows these precepts can dispose up to $4 million or $5 million annually in a manner that demonstrates how little he or she cares about material things." It is at once amusing and revealing when Brooks determines that, for the Bobo, it is laudable to spend a small fortune on a road bike for exercise, but frowned upon to own a powerboat. A jacuzzi is considered too showy, but a slate shower stall is an investment in everyday pleasure. Spending hundreds on caviar? Vulgar. But you may spend the same amount on top-of-the-line garden mulch.

STEALTH WEALTH

What the examples above have in common is visibility. Or rather, their invisibility. Instead of proving something to the outside world, they satisfy an inner need. No one will see an exquisite piece of art hanging in the living room except people invited into the owner's private home. A meal made with imported gourmet salt from Bolivia will be admired by only a handful of dinner guests. Of course, these products are still tokens of status. But they matter only to a select group of insiders. These luxuries are not seen by the general masses, and if they are, do not mean much to them. As a result, they are not open to criticism. They satisfy a very private vanity. Research into the purchasing behaviour of luxury consumers confirms as much. Of those questioned in one study, less than half answered that they "buy products for image reasons". Yet 87 per cent said they were most interested in "the very best quality". This is a high number, even if we take into account that respondents often demonstrate a need for social desirability in such surveys. We call wealth that stays undetected by the general public "stealth wealth", and it is something that could provide good opportunities to luxury companies. After all, they stand for attention to detail, craftsmanship and the kind of excellence demanded by customers who want to buy something that's more than a mere product.

TELLING STORIES

In the previous chapter, we mentioned Hermès as an example of a company taking new initiatives in the Asian market. What the brand has traditionally done very well is to make sure the product is worthy of its logo – in other words, valuing craftsmanship, even when this means going out of the way to find artists whose vision is appropriate for the brand. The famous Hermès scarf was first created in 1937. Some of the most popular designs the company has used are by Kermit Oliver, who then Hermès CEO Jean-Louis Dumas discovered while travelling in the United States in the 1980s. Dumas was taken by Oliver's rich depiction of native flora and fauna. The painter has since produced some of the bestselling designs for Hermès. The coup? Kermit Oliver was not an established artist, but a postal worker from Texas. Here we have a precious material combined with a long history, excellent craftsmanship and the triumph of talent over obscurity. Women like Jackie Onassis, Grace Kelly and Audrey Hepburn, who were the epitome of sophisticated style, all wore Hermès silk scarves. The result is that the brand has had a bestseller for decades.

This kind of brand storytelling captivates customers. Cultured consumers dislike aggressive marketing as much as ostentation itself. If companies want to keep selling to them, they need to find more subtle means of communication. Some companies have already started moving away from brash advertising. Again, take Hermès. The product is the focus of the company's advertising campaigns. They have never used celebrities in media advertising, something that sets them apart from competitors. Another company that has successfully harnessed subtlety is German retailer Manufactum. Under the banner "The good things in life still exist", the company offers handmade and expertly crafted products, often locally sourced and with an appreciation for history. The nostalgia comes with a large price tag, but customers are happy to pay for it. At Manufactum you can find lamps from England that were once used on the ships of the Royal Navy. Or the Danish "Colonial Chair", made from cherry wood in the same cabinetmaker's workshop where the first one was made in 1949. Manufactum also has re-editioned scents from Paul Poiret, the first Parisian couturier to create his own line of perfumes. Manufactum customers are made to feel as though they are not buying a product, but maintaining a heritage. Then, of course, there are the brands that do not advertise at all. Not on paper at least. Their best advertisements are word of mouth and longevity. Prime examples are the tailors in London's Savile Row. Anderson & Sheppard, for instance, can count on their customers to return only because they offer the kind of attention and impeccable work that make the price of a handmade suit seem worth it. And you have to look for their label, discreetly stitched on the inside pocket.

Quality, history and authenticity. Besides bespoke clothing, no other segment of the luxury industry manifests all three better than watchmakers. Patek Philippe is already using them to strengthen its position in the market. "You never actually own a Patek Philippe. You merely take care

Consumer development

Tastes change over time. Meaningful consumption dominates mature markets while ostentation rules in emerging markets.

Know

Mature markets

Meaningfulness

Consumers purchase luxury that engages them mostly on an emotional level. Self-realisation is key.

Knowledgeability

Consumers are passionate about collecting rare items to indulge their sophisticated tastes.

Differentiation

Consumers buy to gratify their sense of elegance and quality, looking to make informed and discerning choices.

Ostentation

Consumers flaunt their wealth, competing with peers for status.

Emerging markets

Show

of it for the next generation," says the advertising campaign alongside a picture of a father and son. In another ad, a mother and daughter are shown with the tagline, "Something truly precious holds its beauty forever". These slogans satisfy a desire for meaningfulness, even if they seem to be clichés. They also legitimise the purchase. Customers do not just do something for themselves by purchasing a watch, but are also thinking of their offspring. Having non-egotistical motives is something that appeals to modern consumers. Infographics on pages 96 and 98 better illustrate consumer buying motivation.

GROWING SOPHISTICATION

It would be easy to assume that the emerging power players are still in the ostentation stage of the consumption cycle. After all, they have only experienced wealth in recent years and are drawn to the flash of popular brands. However, the fast growth of the market outlined in the chapter "East is the New West" has accelerated the sophistication of the emerging market.

Wealthy Chinese consumers are swiftly developing a taste for refinement. In 2012, two-thirds of Chinese consumers said they preferred luxury items that were understated and low-key. In 2010, it was only half. Similarly, more than one-half of shoppers felt it in bad taste to show off luxury goods in 2012, one-third more than in 2010. This is now equal to the statistics from Japan. What is intriguing about this is that Japanese consumers have been exposed to luxury for much longer. Markets develop at different speeds. Something else for companies to consider is that while there is a truth to every cliché, that truth is never the whole story.

FULFILLING ASPIRATIONS

With the different developments at play, it will be interesting to observe how companies bridge the divide between the newly moneyed and the established wealthy without losing customers. There is something they should keep in mind as they attempt to do so. As an expert of the luxury

How much more do I need?

The basis for luxury shopping decisions differs a lot around the world. While Germans feel they have many material desires fulfilled, the Chinese would still like to have more stuff.

Material desires fulfilled

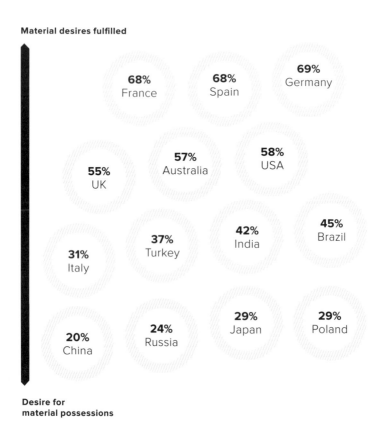

**Desire for
material possessions**

Source: World Bank

field once said, "If it's not credible to an expert, it's not aspirational to the novice." As luxury becomes more widely available worldwide and to different classes and ages of consumers (a subject we will address in depth in our following chapter), the elite will always be ready to pay for even more distinction. The person buying a Porsche key ring is most likely not the same person who buys a Porsche. Someone who wears Chanel sunglasses does not necessarily have access to the world of made-to-measure Chanel fashions. For now, it is key to remember that true luxury often lies in limitation. Limited editions and unique products have proven successful for brands as varied as Dries Van Noten, which let shoppers design their own dress in a one-time-only event, or Montblanc, which offers customers the chance to create their own writing instrument with their designers. Similarly, limitation is key to the success of The Row, a fashion label created by Mary-Kate and Ashley Olsen. The person walking down the street behind an owner of an alligator-skin backpack might mistake it for just another leather bag. But the person wearing it will know that it cost over $39,000, and that they are one of a few people on the planet who have one. The Row's backpack sold out almost immediately after it hit the shelves of high-class department stores.

Looking beyond outward appearances, these customers also want to show that they can afford the kind of luxury that goes deeper. Yes, they could afford a sports car that costs half a million. But they would rather spend it on solar panels to heat their outdoor pool. Investing in sustainable luxuries, products that will make the buyer feel good, and do good at the same time, is a fairly recent development that deserves extensive analysis. We look at this in chapter eight. For now, we can establish that less on the outside represents greater value for modern luxury shoppers. This is good news for the brands trying to secure their commitment.

CASE STUDY
How understatement works
for Victoria Beckham

Everything about it was bling. A pop star marries a top-money professional football player. The duo jet-sets around the world, looking as good in paparazzi photos as in advertising campaigns. David and Victoria Beckham.

No wonder someone eventually asked Victoria to put her name on a clothing line. Even if she needed support to design, any marketer knows she is a moneymaker. Her role as a mother and her openly discussed marital problems endeared her to women of all ages.

But many were surprised when the line was launched in 2008. They were even more surprised by its success. The clothes feature the same simple look which is her signature on the stairs of a private jet, leaving a private club or even shopping with the kids.

Victoria Beckham boutiques are intentionally low-key. Often you cannot see the name until you peer inside the door. The locations are understated too: Bahrain, Australia, Canada, Austria, Azerbaijan, Belgium and China. Her first London outlet was only expected to appear in 2013 and her online presence began in the same year.

Beckham said she worked for three years to get the website to reflect the look of her stores. Her new website also acknowledges the impact of online shopping. Her Icon brand is only available online, and she includes Instagram and other intimate snaps of her life to pique interest. We discuss this further in chapter five.

The brand's success is anything but low-key and recently landed her on BBC Radio 4's list of the most influential women in Britain.

The Victoria Beckham look
The former Spice Girl has created a brand that draws on
subdued design and simple lines, as displayed by this model.

"Increasing education brings more customers."

An interview with Anders Thomas,
CEO of Porzellan Manufaktur Nymphenburg,
which has been making porcelain at the
same site in Germany since the 18th century.

Is luxury consumption moving in the direction of inner values, and as a result, is it becoming increasingly less conspicuous?

We are seeing a trend that people want to buy quality that has authenticity, and this is a contradiction to so-called "bling-bling" luxury. In this respect, you gain a certain amount of authenticity with craftsmanship, real value-creation. You produce a luxury item that sets itself apart from industrially manufactured products that with lots of marketing can get tagged as being luxury. Customers today are more selective and are taking a look at the true value behind a product.

Why is that?

I think it's because many customers who have the financial means are looking for a product that their neighbours can't buy, because it's just not available on the mass market. You would like to own a product that, by the choice of the brand, is signalling connoisseurship.

Why are Nymphenburg products an example of this?

Anyone who buys our products has this connoisseurship. With porcelain, we are part of the third pillar of the luxury market. The first is made up of products you wear: watches, jewellery, clothing, sunglasses, shoes or handbags. The second is products which are also visible to everyone. Your car, home, maybe a boat. But I only let others see the third pillar when I invite them home for a dinner and take out my tableware. The external impact we have as a luxury product is very low-key, but at the same time we are especially important. Someone who is familiar with porcelain can immediately see whether it's Nymphenburg or another brand. Every métier has its connoisseurs and I believe porcelain is experiencing a renaissance among them right now.

When referring to the maturity of luxury markets, we speak of four stages of luxury. The first stage involves "ownership orientation", then comes "differentiation", then "knowlegeability" and finally "meaningfulness". Where do you see yourself here with your products?

Probably somewhere between three and four. Someone who buys a service from us for €200,000 usually likes to express their personal wishes to us. Anything from their initials to elaborately crafted portraits of family members. Or drawings of the 15 manor houses they own. We're already way beyond "differentiation" here, in places where people are searching for meaning. And this is where the trend is headed in the luxury sector: towards values and culture, in this case the culture of dining. People now say, "I want a leather bag that was hand-sewn by one craftsman who completed all the steps himself, starting with the initial cutting to the finished bag." At the same time I'm buying a story, an emotion, a personal connection, which is reflected in the product. I become part of it.

Are you in international markets that place more emphasis on status, and less active in developing markets?

This has a lot to do with education. Our customers are more versed in history and craftsmanship than average customers. This type of customer can be found in every market. We have Asian, Russian, Arab and American customers. And across the board, they all place orders at the highest level. Of course their preferences slightly vary. One might like more opulence and gold. Another, a little more red. Still another likes things a bit more classic or minimal. But basically, our customers always have the same standards for the product, art and design.

Customers who have the financial means are looking for a product that their neighbours can't buy, because it's just not available on the mass market. You would like to own a product that, by the choice of the brand, is signalling connoisseurship.

But what's it like in China, where the market is still in a relatively early stage of development. Isn't it true that customers who have more refined tastes and knowledge are more likely to find their way to your products?

That's true. I gain more customers the more I educate them. At the same time, customers in China are searching for authenticity, as it's lived in Europe. So I see no need of a different marketing strategy than in other regions, except for adapting the language.

On your website, there is an exclusive login area. Can you tell us what's behind that?

This is the area dedicated to our project business, in other words, bespoke products. If you want to choose a very specific shade of blue for your villa, for example, we will develop it for you. Or, for when we design a new decor for a yacht. Customers can log in there and take a look at how their project is coming along. From the development stage through to production in the lathe shop, moulding shop and so on.

Is this an innovative way of creating loyal customers through the use of digital technology, something which wouldn't have been done before? Or is this something that was always in place, only now it's a different platform?

Previously, we had local customers, now we are increasingly more international. We sold tableware to China 40 years ago, but back then it was most likely a service from our classic repertoire. Today, I'm selling tableware in

I gain more customers the more I educate them. At the same time, customers in China are searching for authenticity, as it's lived in Europe. So I see no need of a different marketing strategy than in other regions, except for adapting the language.

They don't have to have the feeling they're something special.
They are special because they value the finer things in life.

China which is tailored to the needs of our customers. This is why I need to communicate with them. And I do it online so they can observe the product's course and also see its development. From start to finish, they'll receive uploaded photos from our workshops documenting the course of the production. If they don't have the time to visit our factory, that is.

That sounds quite technical. Isn't there also an emotional aspect? I'll feel like I'm getting special treatment because I have access to a closed area that doesn't allow just anyone in?

This is exactly why these customers don't buy other products which are visible. They want custom-made, unique pieces. That's why they don't want what is being created made public. Later on it will be presented to their friends and acquaintances. They don't have to have the feeling they're something special. They are special, because they value the finer things in life without having to flaunt it in public.

In your opinion, how has the luxury market changed over the past five years, and what can we expect in the next five?

Customers are becoming more established and want to pass on the story of the products they're buying. That's why they're looking for something special. The brands of the big luxury companies that open up shops and offer the same products with different pricing in every place where money is there to be spent, they are the ones who are going to lose their allure.

Because they're too visible, too accessible?

There's over-saturation going on. Either I have to artificially make the product scarce, like the Kelly bag, where I have to wait three years before I can

Customers are becoming more established and
want to pass on the story of the products they're buying.
That's why they're looking for something special.

finally get one in red. But apart from that, these products are ultimately interchangeable. I think the trend is heading towards individualisation. I see that very strongly with us. If I went to the Kruger National Park and photographed 25 animals, then I'm going to like to have them painted on 25 different plates and also my wife should be everywhere in the background and my kid or my dog, or anyone who was there with me. I want to tell a story. The higher-price mass market will probably still hold up, only because there are enough customers in the pipeline. We're seven billion people right now, in 2020 we'll add on a billion more. 2 to 5 per cent of them will most likely be able to afford luxury products, eventually.

CHAPTER FIVE

THE NEW AGE OF ACCESS

How to capitalise on e-commerce
without losing intimacy
in an era of digital transparency

RETHINKING LUXURY

"The Internet changed everything,"
said designer Dries Van Noten
after a recent fashion show in Paris.
"When you're putting together a
fashion show now, you have
to ask yourself, what will be the first
image that people see online?
Will the print on the clothes be big
enough to see on an iPhone?"
It is a remarkably candid statement,
considering that designers
traditionally want full creative control
of their shows. Says Van Noten,
"In the past, the professional press
wrote the reviews. Then 13- or
14-year-old girls started writing
reviews. You can say that's wrong.
But it's modern times."

Dries Van Noten's open-mindedness here could be rooted in his background as part of the "The Antwerp Six", an avant-garde group of Belgian designers who rose to prominence in the 1980s. They rejected accepted conventions of fashion and marketing. Or perhaps Van Noten is just very clued in to the digital age. Either way, he broached a subject with which many of his fellow designers are struggling to come to terms. Success as a luxury brand no longer depends on pleasing the old guard of money or the professionals judging the collections with trained eyes. The Internet has made luxury consumption more transparent. Today, a company has to reach the future, Internet-savvy generation of shoppers, directly and unfiltered. For example, not many 14-year-old girls in the world can spend €1,500 on a silk-embroidered coat by Dries Van Noten. But they might one day. And until that day comes, their aspirations are part of the conversation about luxury. These are some of the gatekeepers that luxury brands must acknowledge today.

AN OPEN CONVERSATION

Until recently, that conversation was more a private matter. There was a silent understanding between the manufacturers and the buyers, who expressed their appreciation not so much in words as in an exchange of money. If discussions took place, they would be discreet, almost intimate. Think of the tailor on Savile Row measuring a customer, the luxury watchmaker inviting a client to the workshop in Glashütte, the designer making alterations for a woman ordering a couture dress. The once highly personal nature of luxury chit-chat is being drowned out by the clamour of the Internet. And the noise is only getting louder. Global online sales of luxury goods are outperforming the rest of the market in terms of growth. As this progresses, we believe it is vital for brands to make themselves heard. There is money to be made online. The emergence of the Internet has been noticed by the industry. Many companies have understood that they must transfer the luxury experience from the real world to the digital universe. But they are still unsure of how to capitalise on e-commerce without losing the intimacy that once was a hallmark of luxury. The Internet is a great equaliser. Everyone has access. Someone who might not visit a boutique in St. Moritz is two mouse clicks away from looking at the brand's online shop. For a market that is based on exclusivity, democratisation presents a challenge. How do you increase revenue while maintaining a brand's image? The first step is to reach a better understanding of your customers.

For one thing, luxury customers are getting younger. Generation X and Y shoppers, especially in Western countries, are single-person households until much later in life than were their parents. They have only their own wishes and desires to consider when they are spending. Research indicates that they are also more likely than their parents to have been exposed to luxury early in their lives. What they have in common with their predecessors, however, is that they expect their time and money to be valued by the brands they invest in. As we pointed out in chapter four, the post-recession consumer, especially in established economies, is looking for luxury that expresses sophistication. They desire something that is not for everyone.

Keeping these demographic changes in mind, we believe that brands must also consider a second development shaping the market: the near ubiquity of personal computers, tablets and smartphones among luxury consumers. They were able to afford the devices before anyone else, and have consequently moulded their lives around them. Research among affluent consumers in the United States has shown that 98 per cent of them shop online already, spending five hours per week on e-commerce websites and on average $3,700 every three months on orders. Interestingly, nearly half of those consumers use mobile devices to shop online, and the highest percentage of these are consumers under the age of 45. This development is likely to spread to emerging economies, as the global market for smartphones is rapidly growing. Some 2.4 billion PCs, laptops, tablets and smartphones were sold worldwide in 2013 and, by 2016, tablets and smartphones will outsell PCs and laptops. Being online will be part of everyone's reality, not just current luxury shoppers. To appeal to an Internet-savvy luxury consumer, brands will have to offer more than a directory of online shops on their websites with the hope that visitors will navigate their own way to the products. Instead, companies should start viewing the Internet as something that can add to the experience of buying luxury rather than something that will diminish the brand. They should keep in mind that the majority of people who regularly buy luxury goods online stay loyal to their preferred brands on the Internet.

Certainly, online cannot offer everything available in a boutique. The grandeur of a shop's interior, the handle of an expensive fabric, the gleam of a gemstone – these qualities are impossible to duplicate. In chapter six, we will look further into the power of walk-in shops. But luxury has always also stood for innovation – a word that immediately comes to mind when thinking about digital lifestlyes.

TIME FOR CHANGE

Considering the old world aura of Swiss watch brands, it is perhaps surprising that they were some of the first luxury products to go online. For our case study on pages 114 and 115, we selected some of the most convincing technological novelties by watchmakers. For now, we want to focus on one specific example. Vacheron Constantin, a famous name from the world of haute horlogerie, offers customers access to The Hour Lounge, a digital forum where enthusiasts can share their love and knowledge of fine watchmaking. The Hour Lounge delivers something that luxury consumers treasure: the feeling of being knowledgeable and informed. It also is a convenient way to attract customers who want access to this exclusive world. The forum grants that wish, and at the same time acknowledges the brand loyalty of existing customers. The success of an experiment like this remains to be seen.

We believe that appealing to the gatekeepers, those consumers who get first access and then spread the word, is a smart way for brands to be part of the conversation, but also to dominate the way in which the brand is discussed. Research suggests that wealthy shoppers almost uniformly agree that buying online does not devalue the luxury experience. Many of them would like their favourite luxury brands to have an excellent online presence. Another study found that close to three-quarters of luxury product consumers do not set a limit to how much they will spend on online purchases. For these consumers, time really is money. The more convenient it is for them to access their favourite brands online, the more likely they are to spread their wealth.

Continued on page 116

INFLUENCERS
Luxury watch companies are leading the way
in digital innovation with smart-looking apps

In the luxury sector, watchmakers were among the first to embrace apps for their customers. Perhaps it was because of their historic interest in innovation. But they haven't taken long to get it right. Not long ago it was as if a different watchmaker was unveiling a new app every week. And the apps themselves were often unique, going beyond mirroring what was already available in print or online. Watch app fever eventually spread beyond manufacturers to watch publications and enthusiasts. Regardless of whether the app originates with a manufacturer or an aficionado, they are all good for the watch industry.

Jaeger-LeCoultre

Creating an app can be simple. It has become a rite of passage for first-year computer students. However, developing a useful, innovative app requires commitment, imagination and courage. Jaeger-LeCoultre set the bar high with one of the first watch apps in 2009. Taking advantage of the format's multimedia capabilities, the company offered a digital version of its current catalogue and also provided six brief tutorials in watchmaking. The tutorials had little value beyond their first viewing, but they offered fans and owners something new and created a buzz for the brand.

Effective apps like the one from Jaeger-LeCoultre must offer something more than a digital version of a brand's portfolio.

Girard-Perregaux

Good apps must offer something other than a digital version of a brand's portfolio. When they do, they not only attract the attention of loyal followers, but also act as brand ambassadors. Girard-Perregaux added a new twist to the watch app mix. You can take a picture of your wrist, and let the app enhance it with an actual Girard-Perregaux model of your choice. Neither this nor the Jaeger-LeCoultre app seems particularly modern or revolutionary, but both are a step in the right direction. They use innovation to move app technology forward and get the word out about their exceptional brand. They do not settle for a simple app reflecting marketing material that can be found elsewhere. They create something different.

Linde Werdelin

Finally, Linde Werdelin went somewhere completely different. It offers its fans a ski-guide app that taps into GPS information to help users find restaurants, slopes and hotels. The app is special because it gets the brand's message into a space one would not expect to find it. Customers think of their watches while trying to find the best place to ski.

THE CUSTOMER ADVANTAGE

Showcasing the uniqueness of a product online is an important selling point. But another vital aspect of shifting luxury goods online is providing an excellent selection. Fashion and footwear have the highest presence of any luxury goods sector online. Given these overwhelming numbers, we want to highlight one of the Internet's success stories. Net-A-Porter, the multi-brand online store for luxury women's clothing and accessories, was founded by entrepreneur Natalie Massenet in 2000 and has since been acquired by Richemont. The company has demonstrated acumen in addressing two questions that determine the success of any luxury brand online. First, what is the customer's advantage in buying from us? And then, how do we gain their trust? Faith in a brand's image is a characteristic of luxury products. Net-A-Porter's unrivaled selection covers over 400 brands, from Alaïa to Yves Saint Laurent, and it often introduces its customers to new labels. In doing so, it provides a range of products that the customer would otherwise never encounter in one shop.

The basics of Net-A-Porter's service are an easy payment process and express deliveries. There is a stylist on hand to help with selections, and the customer receives a personalised note with each purchase. Customised email messages inform the shopper when new stock of their preferred brands have arrived at the warehouse. From the start, Net-A-Porter also introduced collaborations with designers such as Stella McCartney and Alexander McQueen, giving its customers priority access to sought-after goods. Rounding off the Net-A-Porter world is its own online magazine and a big presence on social media sites. For Net-A-Porter, engaging the consumer on many levels while making things easy has been rewarded with great loyalty. The site gets around six million visitors every month. It is very different to the impersonal world the Internet is sometimes made out to be. Being able to compare brands through technology gives consumers an outlet for their curiosity about fashion trends. Even for those consumers who just drop into the site without buying, having this access is an aspirational experience, and one with which they can actually interact. This interaction can enhance the latent appeal of products.

Luxury consumers use the Internet to compare prices, too. The expenditure on "off-price" goods steadily increases year to year, showing that shoppers are interested in e-commerce to gain an advantage in terms of price. Getting a discount or a good deal on a product or service lets them feel like they are getting priority treatment. This is the success behind popular websites for discounted designer goods such as The Outnet, Gilt or Yoox. Brands worried that the "best deal" mentality of the Internet will affect their sales should remember that although luxury consumers are not above comparing products and prices, getting something at a discount is not their primary motivation. Here's a case in point. On Net-A-Porter, the most expensive and exclusive items sell extremely well. Some Balmain jeans sell out almost as soon as they become available, and they cost €10,000. Those who bought them did not expect them to be cheaper just because they were being sold on an online shop.

Net-A-Porter's business model has paved the way for others to follow. Multi-brand online shops such as Germany's Mytheresa and Stylebop are currently reporting annual double-digit growth. Modelling an online store on other's successes can work, but the luxury industry has always been about leading the way. Brands should view the Internet as an opportunity to explore new ideas and ventures. A good example is Moda Operandi. The e-commerce site was launched in 2011 to offer subscribers preferred access to luxury fashion directly from the runway. Registered customers pay a deposit on the goods, reserving them for later in the season. Allowing customers to come first has boosted Moda Operandi's profile. After only its first year, the company received $36 million in funding from companies such as LVMH, IMG and Condé Nast.

REINVENTING A CLASSIC

The success of multi-brand online shops so far discussed depends on establishing good relationships with the brands. However, brands should also consider approaching their customers directly, because this increases control over the brand's image. It sometimes offers an opportunity to redefine that image entirely. Burberry has been much praised for recognising the power of digital early on and using it to its advantage. Under the guidance of former CEO Angela Ahrendts, the brand has given itself a complete makeover.

Burberry was founded in England in 1856 and became known for inventing a new fabric for raincoats. For many years, the brand relied heavily on its famous raincoats. Too heavily. It missed developing more products, and financial problems followed. When Ahrendts took over in 2006, alongside head designer Christopher Bailey, she devised a strategy to create a modern luxury brand for a worldwide market that simultaneously honoured the brand's British roots. The trademark check pattern was retained. Classics like the trench coat were redesigned for their high-fashion line Burberry Prorsum to appeal to younger and more style-conscious consumers. To supplement the new direction, Burberry also invested in its online presence. It was one of the first fashion houses to live-stream a catwalk show. Starting with its autumn 2010 Burberry Prorsum collection, it allowed customers to order items from the runway via an app. The purchases were then delivered before stock reached the shops. Customers were also encouraged to give feedback via the interactive website, the "Art of the Trench", where people could upload pictures of how they wear their trench coats in their everyday lives and on special occasions. The site also featured images from blogger Scott Schuman of The Sartorialist. Burberry's new business strategy culminated in the opening of a flagship store on Regent Street in London, reversing the common business model by transferring the online shopping experience into the real world. Salespeople carry iPads to show customers how a personalised trench coat might look on them. Customers can also order items that might not be in stock or get details on more than 8,000 items on digital displays. We think this is a strategy that needs to be investigated by any brand. We will discuss this further in chapter six.

Burberry has managed to bridge the gap between keeping an exclusive image and improving revenue, and the company's profits have soared under Ahrendts' leadership. Competitors are pursuing the same success. Barbara Rybka, who spent a decade in Silicon Valley before becoming Gucci's digital director, told the magazine *Fast Company*, "If you look at the average luxury shopper, they consume most information through their mobile devices,

Digital presence

Burberry has created a very successful web cosmos that is seamlessly integrated into its real-world stores.

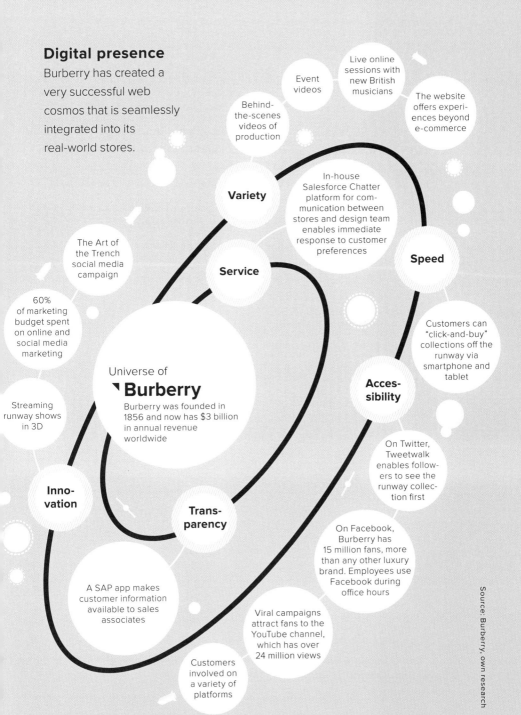

Event videos

Live online sessions with new British musicians

The website offers experiences beyond e-commerce

Behind-the-scenes videos of production

Variety

In-house Salesforce Chatter platform for communication between stores and design team enables immediate response to customer preferences

Speed

The Art of the Trench social media campaign

Service

60% of marketing budget spent on online and social media marketing

Universe of
⟍ Burberry
Burberry was founded in 1856 and now has $3 billion in annual revenue worldwide

Customers can "click-and-buy" collections off the runway via smartphone and tablet

Acces-sibility

Streaming runway shows in 3D

On Twitter, Tweetwalk enables followers to see the runway collection first

Inno-vation

Trans-parency

On Facebook, Burberry has 15 million fans, more than any other luxury brand. Employees use Facebook during office hours

A SAP app makes customer information available to sales associates

Viral campaigns attract fans to the YouTube channel, which has over 24 million views

Customers involved on a variety of platforms

Source: Burberry, own research

The mobile future

Shopping online with mobile devices is becoming more important. By 2017, tablets will be outselling PCs, and an increasing number of consumers will be buying smartphones and ultramobile PCs.

2013　　　　　　　　　　　　　　　　　　　　　　　　**2017**

1,875,774
Mobile phones

2,128,871
Mobile phones

315,229

PCs and notebooks

467,951
Tablets

197,202

Tablets

271,612

PCs and notebooks

23,592
Ultramobile PCs

96,350
Ultramobile PCs

Shipments in thousands of units

Source: Gartner Market Research 2013

even more so than the average smartphone user." Half of Gucci.com's traffic comes from people on smartphones, clicking through from email blasts. After the launch of a new mobile site in early 2013, Gucci's shoppers have proven her right.

The site has brought in far more customers than anticipated. Their mobile conversion rates have increased by 70 per cent, and mobile revenue has quadrupled. These numbers are mainly thanks to the site's simplification of the entire e-commerce experience, from browsing to checking out. Says Mark Lee, former CEO of Gucci, "Our goal is to reach the number one position in luxury online sales in every country." Of paramount importance in reaching such lofty goals is a presence on social media sites such as Facebook, Twitter and Pinterest, which let the customer share information and participate in creating a desire for the brand. The predominantly young audience that spends time on social media is growing year by year, so luxury brands should be encouraged.

MAKING IT PERSONAL

Another way for brands to reach out to prospective customers online is to use a middleman, a different kind of gatekeeper, to deliver their message. Increasingly, luxury brands are approaching bloggers to represent them, offering incentives such as gifts, paid ads or roles as brand ambassadors, which can be problematic as it can compromise journalistic neutrality. The reason behind this is as simple as it is convincing. One of a blog's greatest assests is the personality of the blogger. Readers are likely to buy the products that have the blogger's personal approval. In fact, more than one-quarter of European and American consumers are looking to blogs to help make decisions about brands. That number is even higher in China, where online shoppers put their trust in blogs. Promoting a brand through personality is an approach that fashion brand Oscar de la Renta has used effectively in its OscarPRGirl campaign. Under the moniker OscarPRGirl, Erika Bearman, the senior vice president of global communications for Oscar de la Renta, invites followers on Twitter and Instagram into her world of beautiful gowns, exciting galas and luxurious travel. She quickly

Continued on page 125

From blogger to brand
Chiara Ferragni first ingratiated herself to readers in her Italian blog,
The Blonde Salad. Now fashion companies have taken note of
her celebrity and are working to attach their image to her street cred.
Bloggers are a new item in the marketing toolbox and should
be treated as a mix of journalist and trendsetter.

accumulated a six-figure following on Twitter and Instagram. The way Bearman presents her life leads followers to identify with her and aspire to be like her. It also shows the brand's clothes in the best possible light. OscarPRGirl is a successful strategy to take control of how a brand is talked about.

Providing customers with exclusive information is also the principle behind the Pursuitist website. It was launched by Christopher Parr, a veteran with 15 years experience in luxury digital marketing. "There is a shortage of online destinations for affluent consumers seeking authentic experience," says Parr. "Plenty of cold bling sites exist, focusing on editorial content with ultra premium and inaccessible luxuries. That's the void, and why Pursuitist was created." Followers of the website get inside access to information in various sections, from epicurean pursuits to technology, from green issues to travel. Stories and editorials are created for these sections. Pursuitist is selective in the brands it works with. The brands, in return, reuse the content of the website on their own online channels (for example, through retweets). It is textbook cross-marketing with the consumer in the middle between brand and facilitator. The consumer is never made to feel like they are being pitched.

"Algorithms increase the probability of making a sale."

An interview with Milton Pedraza, CEO of The Luxury Institute,
a marketing consultancy in New York City.

How important is digital communication for luxury marketing today?

It's absolutely critical. Digital communication enables sales teams to develop long-term relationships with people both in the store and beyond. Sales teams can reach out to customers using their digital devices and the information from the customer relations systems to contact customers, send "thank-you notes", follow up activities after the first purchase or send individualised emails. The key point is that this enables sales teams to become radically more efficient and productive in building long-lasting relationships, which applies to both local as well as visiting customers. However, I don't think that the brain will ever be replaced in the luxury world. The knowledge and the empathy of one human being being able to influence another, in this case the customer, will remain essential. Also for maintaining brand loyalty. That's the critical need for digital communication today. Not just in marketing, but also in long-term, profitable relationship-building.

Digital and physical retail are not mutually exclusive, but can benefit from each other?

Yes. This particularly applies to the top 20 per cent of luxury brand customers, who tend to generate around 80 per cent of profits for the brands. The relationship between brand and customer can now be cultivated in a much more effective and efficient way.

Why has the luxury industry been so slow in adopting digital communication?

I think the luxury industry is paradoxical. On the one hand, it is the one industry that has brands spanning across hundreds of years, exhibiting resilience and longevity. On the other hand, the industry is slow to adapt to innovation. While this can be frustrating, I see wisdom in the practice of following certain innovations rather than leading them. In the areas of design, product and store innovation, for example, the luxury industry often takes the lead. But in the area of technology, the industry tends to take a slow, deliberative approach. Yet I don't think it is fair to argue that this has been disadvantageous for the industry. While opportunities may have been missed in terms of timing, the industry eventually has caught up. There is no question that the luxury industry today is selling a considerable amount via e-commerce. However, the relationship-building mindset and execution has to be developed further, to move from a product culture to a customer culture.

What are good examples of luxury brands embracing digital communications?

Bottega Veneta is one of the brands that is doing fabulous things behind the scenes, in terms of relationship-building from the human side. I also think that Burberry is at the forefront in terms of leveraging technology, particularly within the store. But in the case of those companies, a great product obviously is the sine qua non.

Is Gucci's smartphone app that allows you to purchase products a good model for luxury e-commerce? E-commerce has traditionally been met with considerable scepticism.

To me, these kinds of apps are probably the least interesting aspect of technological innovation, because customers will be reluctant to install and use multiple apps for their favourite brands, on top of the range of apps they already use in their daily lives. Mobile websites are of course important, but unless these apps offer a highly individualised and relevant experience, the incentives may not be strong enough for consumers to download and actually use yet another app for an individual brand. Especially wealthy consumers want a personal and visually stimulating experience, which smartphone apps cannot provide.

But e-commerce in luxury is certainly growing.

Absolutely. However, it is the kind of e-commerce that has a strong human component, where experts are able to provide a comprehensive service and engage in dialogue in order to enhance the online experience. This will be the modus operandi of the future.

Do you think this will materialise differently in different places?

There may be slight geographical differences, but Chinese customers in Shanghai or in New York will want the same shopping experience. We are talking about well-travelled, global, in-the-know people, who have certain expectations of luxury brands which are universal in their nature: a great product, an entertaining and logical store as well as engaging, likeable, expert and trustworthy salespeople. Those elements, which we sometimes mistake as culture, have to be delivered regardless of any geographical or logistical circumstances in order to guarantee long-term success.

So there is a future for bricks-and-mortar retail?

Yes, although I do see certain changes. There is no doubt that technology has a considerable impact on certain facets of the industry, such as inventory management. However, there are crucial elements of the customer experience that cannot be replaced by machines. Algorithms will give you a certain lift, increasing the probability of making a sale, but they ultimately only serve to empower or enhance the human being. The Amazon model is an appealing one, but it does not have a human face and therefore does not apply to luxury brands.

Having knowledge of your customer is very important to the luxury industry. But are companies in a position to really be able to use all this data?

Yes, they are moving in this direction, and most brands are installing customer relations management systems. But the quality of the data, and which data you are able to obtain, matters. The data has to be collected intelligently but also in a respectful manner. Crucially, it must involve the consent and the trust of the customer. It also matters how the data is used. If any industry is able to benefit from big data, it will be the luxury brands, because they are relationship-builders.

Let's talk about communication. Luxury has always been about the promise of mystery and exclusivity and much of that has disappeared with the Internet. Is this a positive or negative development for the luxury industry?

It's a great thing. Transparency can only be beneficial. Above all, the creative talents within the industry will have more tools to be creative. The feedback they absorb will enhance their output. Secondly, the real-time dimension will improve the customer's experience. Because these companies, for the most part, are ethical and passionate, this increase in transparency can only be favourable to them. When you are unique, transparency and rapid communication helps you to get your message across. At the same time, it makes you more vulnerable, as mistakes are immediately amplified to the world.

Speaking of transparency: Do luxury brands need to be more sustainable?

Sustainability is a far greater imperative for luxury brands because, for the most part, they are not necessities. Customers tend to have a higher tolerance for unethical companies or products when those fulfil some basic and indispensable needs. Luxury brands need to be impeccable in many ways. They must be ethical and treat their stakeholders well. And they should be environmentally and socially responsible, and give back to those in need.

Mass-market retailer H&M advertises aggressively that it is using organic cotton. Prada does not. Is sustainability not a selling-point for luxury products?

H&M may use organic cotton, but it also produces its textiles in some of the places in the world with the worst working conditions. While luxury brands are also not perfect, they are unlikely to employ that type of production, and instead try to focus on having people who produce great products and giving them good conditions to work in. Compared to most other industries, the luxury industry is aware of the need for social responsibility, and can probably be considered a leader in this field. Its executives, for the most

When you are unique, transparency
and rapid communication help you to get
your message across.

part, are ethical, well-intentioned people. But it also has to be noted that consumers more often than not are reluctant to pay a premium for socially responsible products.

What's your view about old and new gatekeepers? What role do magazine editors play vis-à-vis fashion bloggers?

Again, the only way to deal with this change is with honesty and authenticity. While you have the right to try to influence, fake reviews or fake editorials will ultimately have a harmful effect. Credibility and transparency on both sides must be mantras. Whatever a brand represents and stands for will be amplified across the blogosphere. This is true both when a luxury brand produces a great product, with great design, craftsmanship and quality, as well as when it makes a mistake and tries to cover it up. You cannot run and you cannot hide, and this is a good thing. Transparency is a kind of disinfectant for all industries. Ultimately, this apparent vulnerability will have a positive effect.

If you could allocate the marketing budget of a luxury brand, would you reduce efforts in glossy advertising and do more honest storytelling?

I would not necessarily reduce efforts in advertising, but strive to improve it. Awareness matters. One idea would be to use real but attractive people instead of skinny models. Another idea would be to better leverage the editorial content. It is also crucial to improve direct communication with customers, developing personal and relevant relationships with the top 20 per cent of your clients. Intelligent advertising should also be aimed at winning over new clients. The experience of the store, located in prime locations, remains a considerable driver for marketing.

CHAPTER SIX

WHAT'S IN STORE FOR STATIONARY RETAIL?

The role of real-world shopping
in the digital age

RETHINKING LUXURY

The classic term "bricks and mortar" was given a new lease of life towards the end of the 1990s as the growth of e-commerce led analysts to seek definitions that differentiated between two modes of retail. The buzzword was heard almost nightly on hype-heavy news reports about the rising share prices and soaring fame of Internet companies. Analysts seemed to make endless predictions about the demise of retail stores and the concept of serving customers in offline locations – places made of bricks and mortar.

Analysts argued that online retailers would become so powerful that consumers would soon need to do little more than switch on their computers to buy everything they needed. Delivery services would do the rest. Over a decade later, those prognostications have proven to be misguided. Digital has changed the face of retailing. While it is clear that Internet-based shopping probably will never entirely replace stationary retail, bits and bytes continue to transform the in-store experience. Correctly harnessed, they can help boost sales. Luxury retailers paid little attention to the dramatic predictions. Rightly so. Exquisite boutiques and hyper-personal service have always been hallmarks of the industry. A computer and a broadband connection are inadequate substitutes. Even as there are plenty of opportunities in online shopping for luxury brands, bricks-and-mortar retail will continue to flourish because consumers want to look at, study and become comfortable with a product before buying. They want to get the feel of it in the palm of their hand or gauge the exact fit. Inspecting a product personally, with the service provided by a luxury retailer, is part of the buying experience, especially when it comes to luxury items such as fine china or crystal. Most affluent consumers know more about the products and companies behind them than mass-market consumers, so they are even more anxious to see, feel and experience before they buy. Stationary retail offers both reassurance and instant gratification. For these reasons alone, traditional retail will remain a key component of the luxury business. Clearly many luxury retailers feel the same way. The world's biggest luxury companies continue to open new stores around the globe.

THE NEW RULES OF LOCATION

Finding the right space to match a brand's DNA is the first step in successful traditional retailing, and has become even more important since the Internet increased the familiarity of customers with brands and their products. Stationary retail allows a brand to go where its fans are or create a space where they want to be. Fifth Avenue, Beverly Hills, Paris' Le Marais or Tokyo's Marunouchi. These are all prime locations that cannot be ignored by a retailer who wants to maintain a strong street presence. Local shoppers will see the local stores of well-known brands as a home away from home and feel a sense of pride that their favourite manufacturers deemed their city important enough to have a location. It helps to make consumers feel special and wanted. Retail locations in secondary markets or neighbourhoods that are not so central offer the same, perhaps even to a greater degree. Stores in secondary markets can even be designed to become destination stores or used for temporary events, perhaps alongside an internationally known event such as a horse race, polo match or art show. "Smaller streets boast a higher density of storefronts within a confined space that are targeting the same luxury consumer," says Laura Pomerantz, a founding partner of luxury retailing property consultancy PBS Real Estate LLC. "The stores have more reasonable rents and no attached fees like their mall counterparts, and because this trend is still emerging, prime spaces are available and not yet subjected to overly inflated prices."

Luxury stores must have architecture and décor that resonate with the brand and its identity, interiors that invite customers to come shopping and to linger. Carefully selected artwork and furnishings can reassure customers that they picked the right brand. Customers should be wrapped in a brand bubble within a store. They should get tips for decorating and entertaining from luxury brands. Tom Ford's second Paris store comes to mind, with its beaver rugs and Makassar ebony fixtures. Luxury-store architect Peter Marino commissions artworks specially for projects he is working on. Shoppers should never feel the need to dispense advice on what they would like the next time they shop in a store. Every need should be anticipated. Sales associates are also important here. Sales staff should fit the location and the people who shop there. Multilingual employees are a must. Since we know the Chinese love to shop in Europe, having associates with Chinese is a nobrainer. They also must be familiar with the cultural norms of the customer.

Retail luxury attracts clients, but the stores also serve as advertisements for a brand. Tourists sauntering down Fifth Avenue are there because of the names they see on the storefronts, instantly recognisable from film, TV and literature. Only a tiny percentage of those wandering by the stores have enough in their wallets to buy the products in the window displays. But they see the brands and are reminded of the stories behind the products. The same is true for affluent window shoppers. Brand aficionados might even stop after a few blocks if their favourite brand does not have a presence there, and wonder why. Other shoppers on their way to a specific store might be reminded by a window display of a purchase earlier considered but since forgotten. Stores function as brand ambassadors. Landlords certainly know this, and charge rents accordingly. If you are not where your customers are, someone else will be. Says Piaget CEO Philippe Leopold-Metzger, "When I look at the profitability of the China operation itself, it doesn't really matter. You need to invest a lot in advertising, brand-building and stores because you will get the benefit of it in China and everywhere outside of it with the Chinese." Stores pay for themselves in a variety of ways, not just by what is in the till at the end of the day. Still, rents can get pricey, as shown by the infographic on page 138.

CREATING EXCLUSIVITY

Exclusivity is a key component of luxury. You are unlikely to feel special sauntering into Tiffany's on New York's Fifth Avenue if anyone can stop in for a look. Louis Vuitton is leading the way in the future of stationary retail by not only ensuring its stores are present in key shopping districts (the brand visibility factor) but also by creating unique shopping floors and invitation-only events. Luxury brands know who their customers are and should use the information to create exclusive shopping events and experiences. Above its Bond Street store in London, Vuitton created a private VIP apartment and furnished it with leather couches and artwork from Gilbert & George. Shoppers feel elevated to a higher class of consumer as they are escorted away from the main room. The VIP area has private lounges where shoppers can browse in luxurious surroundings, shielded from prying eyes or cameras. The apartment is furnished like a luxury condo. The concept of a private shopping apartment originated in China, where brands report higher sales in the exclusive showrooms than in their actual showrooms. Although the exclusive spaces can be pricey (analysts estimate the Bond Street apartment cost about $50 million to build) they also bring other benefits. Companies can use the locations to entertain during special events, or for internal events and programmes such as employee motivation schemes. Exclusive suites are also an effective

The world's most expensive retail locations

Luxury retailers are paying high rents for outlets on the most sought-after high streets.

$3,052	**$2,087**	**$1,994**	**$1,325**
New York	**Hong Kong**	**Hong Kong**	**New York**
Fifth Avenue	Queen's Road Central	Tsim Sha Tsui	Madison Avenue

$1,223	**$1,114**	**$930**	**$871**
London	**Hong Kong**	**Zurich**	**Sydney**
Old Bond Street	Causeway Bay	Bahnhofstrasse	Pitt Street Mall

Rents in US dollars, per square foot/year

Source: Colliers International, 2013

tool for dealing with the press. They can enhance a journalist's experience when reporting even a minor story, and turn it into something unique. The apartments can be implemented as the true face of a brand. With private shopping apartments, companies can welcome customers to the inner circle and show other stakeholders how the brand behaves behind the scenes.

Fashion companies have been at the forefront here, often inviting clients to their local store for special viewing events. These offer customers the opportunity to see what is coming in the next season, and a chance to order products while perhaps making another spontaneous purchase. Because events and apartments make customers feel special, they also make them more loyal. We discuss loyalty in greater detail in chapter nine.

Vuitton has perfected the art of unique locations and outdid itself in Asia, where it built a jetty in Singapore and gave its adjacent store a nautical theme to appeal to the shopper who has everything – even a yacht. LVMH, Louis Vuitton's parent company, has been noted for its efforts to craft exclusivity. Vuitton's new retail concepts serve not only as shops but also as global PR tools for journalists to write about. It is a perfect use of an always-on media culture that has permeated every corner.

Other brands are working to expand the concept of stationary retail to offer more than just an experience. They want to create a 24/7 world of luxury in hotels and spas. As mentioned in our chapter on Asia, Armani has a spa in Tokyo's Ginza district, which is also home to Gucci's store and the Shiseido parlour with food, art and a tea room. Extending the experience to other parts of a shopper's life can keep them in the store longer to spend more time – and money – with your brand.

POP-UP SHOPS

Pop-up shops can be very useful to create temporary and surprising urban sales locations. Companies might want to use them to develop a test market or to heighten brand awareness.

Continued on page 142

Location, location, location

Luxury retailers such as Louis Vuitton must pick their locations carefully,
finding unique spaces such as historic London brownstones or
on piers in Singapore. This should be done without seeming to follow
competitors or forcing shoppers to go too far out of their way.

A brand you can walk into

Retail stores are an opportunity to add a dimension
to luxury brands and surround customers
with everything they love about their favorite
manufacturers and fashion houses.

Pop-up shops evolved out of guerrilla marketing early in this century and we still see them as an effective way of leveraging an international event to raise brand visibility and sales. Luxury companies quickly embraced the concept from the start, and should continue to do so. Pop-up shops offer a number of unique advantages. First and foremost, they allow a brand to create a temporary showroom in an unexpected or even normally inaccessible location. A number of brands, such as Montblanc and retailer Saks Fifth Avenue, rushed into Washington DC during President Obama's two inauguration ceremonies to exploit the influx of moneyed admirers. Formula One events, horse races and even industry events can offer similar opportunities. Events keep the attention of attendees for several hours at most, leaving them with free time to shop. By bringing a mini-outlet to the event location, brands can attract customers while preventing them from seeking out other retailers. The latest generation of consumers is accustomed to pop-up shops, so the concept is important. Many modern consumers might even expect seemingly impulsive marketing from their favourite brands.

TO MALL OR NOT TO MALL

On the face of it, there is nothing more pedestrian or non-exclusive than a shopping mall. The whole premise of a mall is to rely on major anchor retailers to lure shoppers who then provide increased foot traffic for smaller, local retailers and restaurants. However, in many areas, malls are the only form of retail, whether it is because a region has grown so quickly, as in Asia, or because of weather conditions, as in the Middle East. Malls become daylong destinations, making them unavoidable in some markets even for luxury retailers. They should be the antithesis of luxury retailing except for one simple fact: all consumers still love the condensed shopping experience offered by malls. Consumers in markets with established luxury shopping areas still seek out the centres, despite having extensive luxury retailing opportunities seemingly around the corner. Consider the The Mall at Short Hills just an hour from Manhattan, New York. There is also the Beverly Center in the heart of Beverly Hills. Hermès itself only recently opened a boutique at the Short Hills mall, putting the brand at the same address as such downmarket mall favourites as California Pizza Kitchen, the Gap and Brookstone. "High-quality regional malls continue to be alive and well," says Robert Taubman, CEO of US mall specialist Taubman Centers Inc.

Malls in Asia are taking on a different flavour, in part because the market is growing so rapidly, and also because there is no alternative. Luxury malls are becoming a destination not only for locals but also for wealthy tourists and travellers. They offer brands a simplified opportunity for entering a new market, albeit with the extra expense and contractual obligations of locating in a mall. Still, brands benefit from the magnetic power of several high-profile names in one place. Brands opting not to locate in the proper destination may also run the risk of being relegated to secondary status by luxury shoppers disappointed by not finding their favourite products there. As with any location, luxury marketers should consider special events or invitation-only shopping nights to reward and encourage local customers.

TUNE IN, TURN ON AND SHOP

Leaps in digital innovation mean that every aspect of luxury retailing can be improved through the use of online tools and mobile apps. In fact, using what works online can be a template for offline success. The revolution in retail begins before a consumer enters the store, when they learn all they can about a product and what their peers think. Social media is the new water-cooler discussion about the sleekest sports car, slickest shoes and most sought-after watch. Bloggers have replaced dull newspaper reviews and, thanks to the interaction of social media platforms, they offer a more personal, intimate view. Shoppers can also go online to find out if a nearby store has the item they want. Or if it is a department store, where they can compare similar products. On the other end, retailers can harness these queries to ensure they have in stock just what their customers want. They can also send loyal customers special offers and react when repeat shoppers appear in a new location. You can now welcome a New Yorker to your Tokyo store with a special present, for example. This would have been difficult in pre-Internet retailing. There is much talk surrounding location-based retailing apps that push special offers when customers pass a shop. But this can come off as a cheap ploy to lure customers, like coupons from a Sunday paper. "Location-based services must be sensitive to consumers' real interest levels. Pushing irrelevant deals too hard at shoppers will cause people to filter them out," says Mike Milley, former manager of design research and strategy for Samsung USA.

Customers can be greeted by a sales associate armed with a tablet. The tablet can offer exacting answers to probing questions, and tell your employees who the customer is and what they have purchased in the past. Predictive software can also feed salespeople information on products that may interest the consumer. Once in-store, the opportunities for digitally assisted shopping are only limited by what marketing and technical staffs make out of them. Clothing stores can offer instant try-ons with computer scanners and flat-screens. The technology is still developing but is worth considering. Does this dress warrant even trying on? If the answer is yes, it could be good for sales. Statistics show that 67 per cent of shoppers who try on an item buy it. While that is from mass-market retailing, luxury shoppers are even more discerning in their choices. But if the dress fits perfectly, they would be more inclined to buy it. We want to also mention here a similar application for restaurants, not because we think it is entirely applicable to Michelin-rated locations, but because it could serve as inspiration. Restaurants are trying out flat-screen tables that show what a diner's order could look like and even lets them place their order, reducing the number of personnel. This, of course, is not feasible in high-end restaurants where service is a chief component of the experience, but perhaps a virtual tour of a wine cellar could be enjoyable, adding extra information about particular wineries. It is important to keep developing untraditional ideas. After all, experimentation leads to innovation, a hallmark of luxury.

As we point out in chapter five, Burberry has been an early adopter in digital. The brand once invited key customers to 25 major stores around the world. They were presented with an iPad in a Burberry sleeve. They watched the introduction of the company's latest collection on the devices and then browsed through the collection on the tablet, from which they could order clothes. This is just the tip of the iceberg. Consumers today also use tablets and smartphones to scan barcodes or product names to find out more information, place an order or search for the right size. The important part is to minimise the dull scanning process and to accentuate brand interaction and support from employees. Digital should also be used to complement the actual shopping experience. If an item is out of stock, customers could be allowed to order in-store with free shipping to their home address. And shoppers can take advantage of tax-free Internet sales while enjoying a showroom experience. It must be noted that the future of tax-free Internet shopping is in jeopardy; most governments around the world have at least discussed taxing online sales and many have already introduced legislation, so brands should factor this in to their calculations.

We do not agree with those who declare that computers and the Internet mark the end of traditional retail. Certainly, the rapid growth of online sales is impressive, but even the most optimistic estimates put online sales at a fraction of offline sales. That proportion is growing, however. Second, properly cultivated and leveraged, computers and an online presence can support sales, especially of luxury items, because they can vastly improve service and the shopping experience. Retailers can consider shifting some sales online to reduce rents, and move warehouse and supply activities that do not affect product quality to more optimal locations.

"As the Internet creates a more savvy and demanding consumer, the pressure is on for these labels to differentiate themselves with a memorable shopping experience," says Pomerantz. "Bricks and mortar has become an essential component in building this emotional connection to the brand." It is clear that the future of stationary retail remains a profitable one.

INFLUENCER
Céline

It was the smallest of changes, but when Celine became Céline it marked the rebuilding of an old French fashion house into one of the modern luxury market's strongest brands. The accent on the "e" symbolised a new era, instigated by British fashion designer Phoebe Philo when she took over as head of design in 2008. The brand, acquired by LVMH for €412 million in 1996, had been struggling financially for years, unable to find a clear design direction.

Philo had been pursued by the chief executive of LVMH's fashion division, Pierre-Yves Roussel, to help turn around Céline's fortunes. Philo, previously successful as chief designer at Chloé, accepted the job – but only if LVMH agreed to her terms. First came the name change. Next, LVMH shut down 20 of the 100 Céline stores worldwide, cut ties with less-exclusive department stores and stopped producing its handbags in China. The manufacturing was relocated to Italy. Furthermore, the company pulled all remaining inventory from stores, giving Philo a completely clean slate before she unveiled her first collection in autumn 2009.

Now open

Her sleek, simple and refined aesthetic represented a complete overhaul for a brand. Céline started in 1945 with a collection of children's shoes and later expanded into women's clothing. Philo introduced recognisable designs in the shape of three bag lines, keeping the design free of ostensible logos. "I felt it was necessary to establish quality for the brand," Philo said, explaining the drastic changes at the time. "Now that we are establishing that and the top of the pyramid is in place, we can open it out."

The efforts to recreate Céline's image and gain control over its products cost the company €98 million. It was an investment that paid off, even as the price point of the clothes and accessories went up. Trousers for €1,000, shoes for €600 and handbags for €2,000 sold out almost as quickly as Philo could design them. In part, that is a testament to her talent as a designer, but also to her acumen in understanding the luxury consumer.

Céline offers quality products without recognisable logos at limited access for elevated prices. This combination enamoured shoppers to the brand, even as the company decided to forego branching out into the lucrative e-commerce sector. Going against the digital current has established Céline as a brand that consumers want to experience in person, making the stores an exciting destination. In fact, since Philo arrived, Céline has doubled its turnover to €400 million.

On sale

Following the opening of a Céline flagship store in New York, further shops will be opened in Hong Kong, Los Angeles and Paris. The bottom line? While LVMH does not reveal the earnings of individual brands, chairman and CEO Bernard Arnault has singled out Céline's "exceptional results".

Confirming his decision to hire her, Roussel forecasts the brand's income to double again in the next three to five years. Considering the brand's success so far, it seems like a reasonable expectation.

"The principle of scarcity works."

An interview with Jörg Wolle, CEO of DKSH,
a Swiss consultancy that markets and distributes customer brands
alongside its own luxury products in Asia.

DKSH has been active in Asia for 150 years and, among other things, handles the marketing and sales of luxury brands. How do you view the relationship of e-commerce and stationary retail?

The luxury industry simply tried to escape the mega-trend of e-commerce for a long time. When that was just no longer possible, it undertook several initiatives under the motto "if you can't beat them, join them". In our view, the trend to e-commerce will keep growing strongly and its driving force will come out of Asia. In Asia, the average buyer of luxury brands is about 14 years younger than the average buyer in Western Europe and about 25 years younger than in the United States. This means that in Asia, we have younger, very affluent luxury consumers who are net savvy. Not only have they grown up with the Internet, but in countries like South Korea, people are real digital trendsetters.

Is stationary retail going to become less important as a result?

You need both. With flagship stores, it's about presenting the brand experience to the consumer. To make sure that the store isn't just a billboard that's generating losses you are going to need a strong brand that draws people there. It's the old problem of the chicken and the egg. But it's clear, without a strong base in stationary retail where people can handle the products, luxury brands don't work. Customers who are looking for a watch have to be able to feel its weight, or look at the craftsmanship details on a dial or see how it fits. They can't do that on the Internet.

So shops will remain the focal points of brands?

Yes, we see shops as being the place where the aura and the brand experience present themselves to customers. E-commerce simply has an additional multiplier effect. An example is when we took over the watch brand Maurice Lacroix, which is very well-known in Germany. The first thing we did was to invest in flagship stores in Asia, and straight after that, opened two in Berlin. The one on Kurfürstendamm is for Berliners and the other one on Friedrichstrasse focuses on tourists. I was confident that the shops would work in Asia but I wasn't so sure if they would in Berlin.

Within a few months though, the boutiques started turning a profit. After we took over the majority of shares at Maurice Lacroix, we revamped the brand's identity. Through the shops we could communicate our new message, "the time is now", directly to consumers. Additionally, this allowed us to give our resale partners in Germany a point of reference. Because a flagship store is important not only for consumers but also for retail partners.

Did the growth of e-commerce come at the expense of stationary retail? Or is the pie big enough for both?

The pie is big enough and it's growing, at least in Asia. E-commerce doesn't work without stationary retail. Brands need to have a presence in both worlds, especially because of young consumers. We see the digital world as being an extension and ambassador of the brand. A place where you can make your friends aware of a product: "Take a look here at what I've found. Which one do you think you'd like?"

Despite all the enthusiasm for e-commerce, luxury brands have opened more shops in China than anywhere else in the world. Is that due to the size of the market?

At first, it was just about quelling the hunger of Chinese consumers and boosting sales. But the hype has died down, and many brands now realise that quality is a lot more important than quantity. I came back a few days ago from a long trip through Asia. The biggest problem that brands like Gucci or Louis Vuitton have in China is that they've become too popular, and that the truly wealthy Chinese are no longer buying them for lack of exclusivity.

E-commerce doesn't work without stationary retail.
Brands need to have a presence in both worlds, especially
because of young consumers. We see the digital
world as being an extension and ambassador of the brand.

What can be done then?

The principle of scarcity works whether you're Hermès or Ferrari. Every brand and supplier needs to ask themselves: What do I want to be? You can't be all things to all people. Trendsetters are distancing themselves from popular brands again and really want something very specific, something unique.

Too much of a retail presence can be damaging?

Absolutely. You have to decide what you want. We sell writing instruments in Japan made by the German companies Lamy and Graf von Faber-Castell. We have hundreds of sales points and shop-in-shops for Lamy. For Graf von Faber-Castell, we have one single boutique in Tokyo. But this flagship store for the upmarket Faber-Castell brand is a world of its own.

How important are malls, especially in Asia?

Extremely important. While these retail complexes no longer play a role in Germany or Switzerland, and London has perhaps two or three big ones, shopping malls in Japan, Korea, Thailand and Singapore are the strongest player in the luxury business. When I first came to Hong Kong 25 years ago, I wondered why the locals stormed to the malls with their families on Saturdays and Sundays.

And why did they?

Because back then, they were incredibly beautiful environments. On top of that, the malls were air-conditioned and most of the people there had no air conditioning at home. This was a quarter of a century ago.

And now everyone has air conditioning.

The important thing is that customers have remained loyal to these malls over generations. In hot climates you'd rather take a trip to the nice air-conditioned mall with your family than go out jogging. Customers arrive in

*We see shops as being the place
where the aura and the brand experience
present themselves to customers.*

the morning and don't leave again until the evening. They go there to have something to eat, buy new trainers or even a new watch. But you have to offer something in return if you want this kind of customer loyalty. For our brands in Asian malls, we offer special bonus programmes, personalised shopping with a customer-care assistant, VIP dinners and shows in restaurants where different brands have the chance to introduce themselves. The malls in Asia have little in common with their namesakes in Germany and the United States, where many of the products that didn't sell on the high street end up being sold off in them.

What future trends do you see in retail?

Everyone could and should learn from Japan. The salespeople there are often better dressed than their customers, and are highly qualified and can advise you in detail. Sales staff will soon receive better training in other parts of the world so that they, too, will be able to provide customers with more detailed information. We send our top salespeople and customer service watchmakers to visit the workshops of the brands that we sell. These are trends I am seeing in retail. Better training, personalised customer service and individualised advice which lets you experience the brand.

Are loyalty programmes becoming more important?

There are still bonus programmes for basic products, and for our more important customers, they come with loyalty cards, true to the maxim "know your customer". It's becoming increasingly important that you understand your customers, track them and let them know whenever there is news. This trend is mainly due to personalisation. Marketing is going to have to adjust itself more to the customers.

*It's becoming increasingly important that you understand your
customers, track them and let them know whenever there
is news. This trend is mainly due to personalisation. Marketing
is going to have to adjust itself more to the customers.*

Does technology such as data collection play a role?

Absolutely, but it's more in the background. People don't want to be constantly confronted with it. It can be uncomfortable if you're a customer
sitting across from someone entering everything into a laptop or iPad. But
if the consultant jots down the information using a Faber-Castell Perfect
Pencil and only later enters it to a database, it's not so obvious, yet they still
have the follow-up under control.

CHAPTER SEVEN

THE LUXURY EXPERIENCE

How to envelop luxury consumers in
brand attributes to meet demand
for individual experiences and events

RETHINKING LUXURY

In the desert of New Mexico,
serial entrepreneur Sir Richard Branson
and his company Virgin Galactic are
preparing to provide affluent
travellers with the next-generation
luxury experience: commercial space
travel. For $250,000 and after
three days of preparation, one can suit
up, climb aboard the company's
SpaceShip Two and get ready for
takeoff from the futuristic "Spaceport
America", the world's first
purpose-built spaceliner terminal.
The extravagant suborbital
flight also includes several minutes
of zero gravity entertainment.

A couple of hundred well-heeled space enthusiasts have already booked a ticket on Branson's space flights. With commercial space tourism expected to take flight soon, Sir Richard Branson is a poster child for luxury's future: the selling of experiences. According to one study, about half of all the money spent in the luxury market is for experiences. And that spending is growing more quickly than product purchases. It appears that we are finally discovering the answer to the age-old question of what to get for the man who has everything: something they have not experienced before.

The reasons for the shift in taste vary depending on the consumer. Aging baby boomers can now look back on a life of consuming and have acquired nearly everything they ever wanted. With a house full of possessions, they are now trying to get the final kick from their remaining decades. And because they have a historical perspective, they understand the importance of memories. Younger customers have grown up with the Internet and seen increasing value placed on the ability to share thoughts, concepts and experiences. And those with the necessary funds can buy experiences. Finally, maturing markets seem to act like maturing people. As consumers become accustomed to luxury and its attributes such as flamboyant designs or flashy, unmistakable labels, travel, food and other none material luxuries become important.

The future of luxury marketing may become a lot like George Mallory's famous quote about climbing Mount Everest: "Because it's there". Trips to Antarctica. Classes with the undisputed expert in a specific field of art or athletics. These things were certainly possible in the past, but often required the right connections or a staff willing to do the legwork. Today, they are just another cornerstone of the luxury industry. It is hard to say which is transforming the top consumer segment more – the Internet, or the push to experience something special. It could be that they accelerate each other.

It is important to note that while we have spoken much here about service and experience as products, clearly the service industry is not the only part of the luxury sector impacted by the experience push. Every aspect of high-end retailing must now be steeped in experience as much as it is in excellence and exclusivity. Prospective customers want to be surrounded in an emotional experience that showcases a company's branding. Experience, in

Superlative service

The Peninsula Hotel chain has luxury properties in six countries and some exceptional ideas for coddling guests.

More than a room

The Peninsula Hotel develops personal relationships and offers unique experiences to impress customers.

On-board

Guests can experience sailing on the Hong Kong Peninsula's own Peninsula Signal 8 racing yacht.

Creating exquisite travel

The Hong Kong Peninsula has a fleet of 15 Rolls-Royces as well as a helicopter for transfers and tours.

Making the impossible possible

Concierge F. Bigler in New York is known as one of the top 10 in his field — a maker of miracles for guests.

terms of marketing, can still also mean sponsorship. Things like sailing regattas, extreme sports, special wine tastings. The important part is to go beyond traditional sponsoring and make a brand part of the event itself. This way, spectators feel as if they are insiders, viewing the event on behalf of the brand. The Peninsula Hotel chain does this well by allowing guests to ride on the inn's own competition yacht. Other Peninsula services are highlighted in the infographic on page 158.

Estate agents selling multimillion-dollar houses have discovered a unique angle that showcases properties by making them the focal point of a bigger event. The estate agent teams up with a corporate sponsor for an invitation-only event that highlights the sponsor's products and the house itself. The guest list comes from both sides, offering a win-win deal to the estate agent and sponsor. For instance, Coldwell Banker Previews International recently teamed up with Rolls-Royce to sell a US property. Experience may also carry through to the aftermarket to keep customers attached to a brand. Bugatti, for example, organises special tours through Italy for select customers. The owners pilot their expensive chariots to workshops, wineries and restaurants that only wealthy locals normally know about.

FAR AWAY, SO CLOSE

Travel is the most obvious of luxury experiences. The affluent have always been good at spending money on getting to places and ensuring they have the best place to stay once they get there. Travel on every level is on the rise as economies recover, but affluent travellers generally spend about 45 per cent more per trip than their less wealthy counterparts. That discrepancy is likely to expand to an 80 per cent difference in the near future, according to credit card company Visa. Those on a budget prefer booking online while 70 per cent of luxury travellers opt to book through travel agencies. More figures from the study are shown on the infographic on page 161.

While space may be the final frontier, there are still plenty of seldom explored corners of the earth where the well-to-do can find superlative experiences. Although companies such as Branson's Virgin Atlantic and high-profile hotel chains do an exceptional job of catering to an exclusive clientele, we do not see the future of luxury travel in the hands of well-known travel and tourism companies. Consumers are clamouring for much more, and are increasingly savvy thanks to the pervasiveness of images on the Internet and television. Cameras have been all over the earth but most people have not. Luxury travel should now offer customers the opportunity to spend time in remote, exotic locations and in quirky, little-known hotels, lodges or even famous houses. The same is true for in-town stays. The hotel should have a bigger story. The site must have a connection to the city's past and offer the customer a sense that he is paying for exclusive access to a unique story. An unlikely brand has cropped up to dominate this space, redeeming on decades of brand-building and a deep network of specialists: *National Geographic*. Who else would know how best to get into the wilds of Madagascar or the backwoods of Canada? The magazine has been going there for years and now it is happy to take you with them for a price. They will even send along one of their famous photographers or scientists to help make your trip memorable.

National Geographic also taps its experts to assemble the trips to ensure participants get the most from their visit while making as small an impact on the locals as possible. Ecological tourism is playing a key role in travel. Como Shambhala resorts play up the eco aspects of their private island locations and promote them by hinting that they care as much about the environment as about their guests' spiritual well-being. Ignoring the carbon footprint of air travel, plenty of sustainability-minded resorts are popping up around the globe to cater to those who demand exceptional service alongside environmental protection. Even if a company does not use sustainability as part of its business plan, keeping consumers informed about efforts to lessen the impact on the earth makes good business sense in any market. "Hotels today must know where they are buying their cleaning supplies or where their food comes from," says Design Hotels founder and CEO Claus Sendlinger. "Our goal is to actually make a difference and, naturally, let people know about it. I think consumers can actually differentiate between hotels that just do something for their image and those that truly mean it."

Travel spending going places

Affluent travellers are increasingly paying much more for
a single trip than other travellers.

$4,501
Next trip

$2,501
Next trip

$2,501
Next trip

$3,465
Last trip

$1,708
Last trip

$2,390
Last trip

**First-time
traveller**

**Typical
traveller**

**Affluent
traveller**

Source: Visa

The major players in luxury have never feared entering a new market or a
different, unfamiliar territory. Travel is no different. LVMH has kicked off
its new ultra-luxury hotel chain Cheval Blanc with two locations, a chalet
in Courchevel in the French Alps featuring interior designs by Sybille de
Margerie, and a second in the Maldives, equipped with beach villas, a tropical garden and a team of experts who specialise in creating customised
experiences for travellers such as diving trips. Bulgari has also created
jewels of tourism around the world. The Italian luxury company operates a
spectacular resort in Bali, located on a plateau on the southern part of the
Jimbaran peninsula, directly adjacent to the sea. Luxury travellers can rent
several villas that provide unobstructed views of the Indian Ocean. At the
resort's Bulgari boutique, guests can shop for new items. Bulgari also owns
an exclusive hotel in Milan and Italian-themed restaurants in Japan.

Luxury hoteliers are also considering new variations on wellness treatments, such as courses on how to deal with information overload in the digital age. Some offer the services of clairvoyants. The trend is for introspection rather than extroversion. "We've now got a psychic in Tulum who can measure global energy fields," says Design Hotels' Sendlinger. "Of course, you can only offer this kind of thing if customers are interested in it. There are plenty of specialty hotels that people book to take a closer look at themselves."

Another trend in luxury travel is the back-to-basics holiday, often on some kind of secluded island. Companies such as Docastaway offer a desert island experience where you can choose between comfort mode and adventure mode. In the latter, guests might have to source their own food from the surrounding landscape while sharing a forest with a native tribe, or combine their holiday with survival training. With private villas and discreet mini-hotels, comfort mode caters to those who "wish to have an experience similar to that of a castaway, but desire certain levels of luxury in order to enjoy their private island vacation," according to the company's promotional copy.

FAMILY FRIENDLY

Families are often seen as status symbols. High-profile super moms and progressive attitudes towards parenting have changed the perception and expectations of family life. Marketing for the demanding family can now be lucrative. Many luxury hotel chains have already embraced this. They go beyond offering simple parent-friendly services such as in-room cribs, babysitting and kids' meals. Four Seasons hotels cater to children, often with child-sized robes, welcome presents and special educational packages. Need a toothbrush for your three-year-old? Just ask. The Waldorf Astoria in Naples, Florida, offers couples amenities such as golf, tennis and a sandy beach with trained counsellors for wealthy offspring. And there are the Atlantis resorts in the Bahamas and Dubai, full of marine animals, dolphins and water slides.

Providing an experience for children is another way to exploit the changing status of families. Red Carpet Kids in Manhattan has several different packages that will keep between 12 and 15 children entertained for an afternoon and free parents from throwing a party. The philosophy behind their parties is to make children feel special with a red-carpet event, including photographers and a doorman who keeps out the uninvited. The content varies – improvisation lessons from a professional thespian, a movie viewing or even a faux Academy Award with make-up, paparazzi and an awards ceremony. All come with a customised cake, treats and kids' food favourites, like chicken fingers and pizza.

Marketing services designed specifically for children can be tricky. Every parent is wary of insincere marketers trying to get to their purse strings through their hearts. Most parents have seen more than a few scam attempts. Sincerity is the only true way to win over parents. The experiences must be based on a true understanding of what children and young adults want as well as the expectations of their parents. Companies must also be able to communicate their deep expertise in this area.

CREATING EXPERIENCE

Experience isn't just for service companies. Product producers also have to deliver an experience. The experience should be about sharing expertise related to the product. Companies must provide their connoisseurs with "connaissance". Alfred Dunhill has embraced this concept in its four new locations, in Tokyo, Shanghai, Hong Kong and London. The label finds extraordinary real estate in sought-after locations and then converts it into clubs, which they call "homes".

They are places where customers come to hang out and do more than spend money, where they completely experience the brand. There are bars with TVs, tailoring rooms to give customers exactly what they want and even movie theatres. The "homes" include memorabilia from the founder to truly ensconce customers in the Dunhill world. The company schedules themed parties and invites leaders to hold talks. At a Dunhill "home", it might be easy for customers to forget that a new shirt was the reason they came in the first place. The Dunhill experience hints at the way to adapt existing retail space to this new need for experience: add meaning.

Stores can also try to find a spiritual, environmental or charitable edge. Hosting a debate with local thought-leaders can help position a brand among the speakers' fans or attach a progressive, contemplative note to a well-known product. Several stores such as Merci in Paris are having success by offering luxury wares while promising the profits to charity. We are not promoting non-profits here, but it is an idea that can be adapted. The important thing is to hand customers a unique storyline about the surroundings. As with marketing to children, the motivation also has to be genuine. A company's goal must be to tie the specific store closer to the address and show an interest in community, despite the exclusive nature of the business. "There is a marketing goal ultimately," says Patrizio di Marco, president and CEO of Gucci. "Definitely the long-term goal, given our continuous and consistent commitment to responsibility, will enhance the brand reputation and, as such, the brand will have more meaning of craftsmanship. Consumers will buy more into the brand besides the tangible values."

German airline Lufthansa is also making frequent travellers feel special with its HON Circle programme. The name combines the familiar three-letter signifier for airports with a shortened form of the word "honour". HON Circle members win half-a-dozen free upgrades just by qualifying and are given access to the airline's exclusive first-class building in Frankfurt with its extravagant buffet, five-star beds and luxurious bathrooms. Members get a special luggage tag that serves no purpose other than to signify to Lufthansa staff, and other HON members, that they belong. The programme effectively singles out those who spend the most at the airline and provides them with incentives to keep flying. To qualify, customers must accumulate 600,000 miles in two consecutive years. HON status can not be bought. The scheme surrounds members in the first-class image the company wants to project and even shuttles them to their flights in a Porsche or Mercedes. The Lufthansa HON Circle experience can start hours before members board, and can continue long after they have reached their final destination.

REWARD YOUR CUSTOMER

This is nothing new to the luxury industry, but it is one simple way to create a unique experience for a client accustomed to unique experiences. In the near future this will be all about intelligent data management. Customers will be in charge of their own online travel profiles, and will grant select hotels access to them in exchange for exceptional treatment. "I want to be recognised as a guest. And when I come back, I want to be treated specially. I do not need a red carpet. Most people do not want one. But if I arrive with my dog and in my room there's a water bowl with his name on it, wow!" says Design Hotels' Sendlinger.

The right salespeople can sense a customer's taste and know which scarf is the appropriate gift for what kind of occasion. The sales associate's knowledge and familiarity, coupled with respectful distance, should be yet another extension of brand identity and the experience a brand offers.

Car manufacturers were some of the first to offer this kind of experience based on their product. American auto enthusiasts have for years sung the praises of European delivery services from the likes of Porsche and BMW. After ordering a Porsche in the United States, buyers fly over to Stuttgart or Leipzig to take delivery. They get to know the car at top speed on the autobahn before dropping it off at a northern European port for shipping back to the States. Porsche is also now building a test track at its US headquarters in Atlanta, Georgia, where buyers who do not want to fly to Europe can try out their new purchase.

Product manufacturers need to leverage their existing strengths to offer their customers what used to be known as value-added features but now count as experience. High-paying customers want to be treated as such and be allowed in the back of the shop. Bugatti does this with its "atelier" for the Veyron model in Molsheim, France. Swiss watchmakers are also veterans in guiding tours through the plant. Creating a superlative experience should not be difficult for luxury companies because the companies themselves are a superlative experience.

Furnished for first-class lounging
Lufthansa's HON Circle First Class Lounge at Frankfurt
International Airport offers a wide range of services, including
chauffeurs to whisk members directly to their flights.

The privilege of privacy

HON members have access to first-class lounges with amenities that
include bedrooms and spas. The HON luggage tag (second image)
discreetly broadcasts the member's status to those who need to know.

HOW TO...
Soho House

When Nick Jones opened the first Soho House in London in 1995, he envisioned it as a private meeting place for his creative friends. Almost 20 years later, Soho House is a powerful worldwide brand. There are branches in New York, Los Angeles, Toronto, Berlin and Miami. It spans the globe with a network of successful influencers who enjoy the luxury of belonging to a closed society. How did Jones establish the Soho House experience?

1. Find the perfect place

In each city, the Soho House is located at the heart of things, easy to reach, with access to cultural offerings right on the doorstep. Often, the house is set up in a historical building, furnished to perfection, with an interior evocative of a grand British mansion. From the foyer to the rooftop, a Soho House experience is built on private luxury.

2. Create the perfect guest list

Only members and their friends are allowed. How do you become a member? It helps to be part of the creative class and successful in your field, but money does not necessarily buy access. Rumour has it that applicants who try to bribe their way in get banned for life. That's a delicious bit of gossip that serves to increase the demand. Annual membership fees range from €1,200 for a Local House to €1,500 for the Every House, a sum luxury consumers might normally spend on a handbag or suit. The fact that money really is secondary only heightens the desirability of membership. The wait for Soho House New York can be as long as a year. Once the applicant gets in, they truly feel like the experience is custom-made for them.

3. Offer exclusivity

Members can make use of the full service of the facilities, including a restaurant and bar, often with a rooftop pool, a fitness club and spa, and a cinema. In the hotel, rooms and apartments are available to members at discounted prices. It is a hotel but more personal. A home away from home for the traveller who is used to flying between New York, London and Berlin, but who can check in to a familiar place in each city, welcomed as a valued member of the club. Part of the service is the privacy each House affords its members. Phones and cameras are not allowed, making it easier for famous guests to move around as though they were in their own home.

4. Set your own rules

Soho House might be modelled on the classic gentlemen's club, a private haven for the well-connected, but it comes without the stiff upper lip. Jones's favourite dress code is jeans and T-shirt. That does not look like luxury? Quite the opposite. The luxury for members here is that they can be who they are, without pretence or putting on airs.

Not for everybody
An empty rooftop pool is a rare sight at the Soho House in
New York City. The house is usually packed with hundreds of members.
Waiting to become a member can take a while.

"There's simply no app for emotions."

An interview with Bernhard Maier,
member of the executive board and head of the sales
and marketing division at Porsche AG.

How is the brand experience changing in an age of increasing digitalisation?

This is best explained by the so-called "customer touchpoint map". We see some modifications here, but some shifting as well. Based on our contact history, we can see how many times interested parties visit a Porsche centre before they sign a sales contract with us. In the past, a Porsche buyer would make five or six visits beforehand to learn about various models and options. In recent years, this number has been decreasing. The reasons for this are an increase in digitalisation and the around-the-clock availability of information. Today, a potential buyer finds a lot of this information on the Internet. So people come to the dealership having very specific ideas in mind. But this need not be a disadvantage. Especially when you can influence the customer's digital touchpoints.

But they're still coming by to have a look?

Yes, but instead of the five or six times, it will be only two or three visits. Because there are a lot of things that a computer will never be able to replace. There's simply no app for emotions. For instance, how it feels to sit in a Porsche, the smell of its fine leather, taking in its ambience. Or during a test drive, experiencing its driving dynamics and feeling the butterflies in your stomach.

Are you seeing changes in your physical showrooms because of digitalisation?

Yes, this is happening. A customer configures and saves their desired vehicle on the Internet. Each configuration receives a Porsche code. The customer comes to us and says: "I made a change on the Internet, and now I'm not quite sure if it was registered. Can you help me?" The salesperson at the Porsche centre can respond with: "Dear customer, do you mean our offer from 23 March? Where you configured a 911 in dark blue with a leather interior?" The salesperson calls up everything on a screen and can then say, for example: "Let's take a quick look at this car's configuration. To really make this your dream car, your most personal car, I recommend..."

We know from current market surveys and Internet analysis that the buying and ownership experience is especially important in the luxury goods sector.

This is effective because it saves time, is emotional and it works with images. These are exactly the kind of tools that we're already using in some of our markets today. And we're working hard to provide this feature everywhere.

So dealerships aren't obsolete. Customers still visit to buy?

I'm firmly convinced that with a product of this quality and price range, the final buying decision is not going to be made on a computer. We know from current market surveys and Internet analysis that the buying and ownership experience is especially important in the luxury goods sector. Customers view a product's exclusivity as being just this point. It can't only be accomplished digitally because personal service is the deciding factor.

If anything, the showrooms and dealerships have to be upgraded even further...

That's exactly the point. We know that the number of visits tends to be decreasing. Therefore, you have to win over customers in a very short time using flawless personal contact. And it has to have all the emotion that they expect.

Is the experience involved when buying a luxury product becoming increasingly important?

You could say that. Besides rational reasons for making decisions such as quality, retaining value, longevity and safety, there are many critical emotional reasons for deciding to buy a product. These include associative values like company image, product design, the personal driving experience

*Many of our customers would like to be engaged
with beautiful and interesting things.
So we invite them to panel discussions, lectures,
gallery openings and other cultural events.*

and the community, which is especially important too. Particularly in saturated markets, people are searching for new experiences, for things previously unknown and unexpected. This is why an experience like the Porsche Travel Club, which we've been offering for many years now, is becoming increasingly important. We also have a Porsche Sport Driving School at our factory in Leipzig and our Porsche Driving Experience Centre at the Formula One Silverstone circuit in England, and we're building three more: one in Shanghai, which is also at the Formula One circuit there, and two more in Atlanta and Los Angeles in the United States. The experience of sports car driving tailored to each customer is one of our distinguishing features.

Could it be that luxury customers are finding the experience increasingly more important than owning something?

Fortunately, our customer base distinguishes itself from others. We cater to everyone, from 18 to the over-80s. The over-50 target group, as well the ones below it, is growing, and this is due to the fragmentation of markets and segmentation of customer groups. In addition, Porsche is no longer represented in 70, but in over 125 markets. And we not only have two, but five model series. Many of our customers still find ownership important. We call them the "Proud Patrons". After breakfast in the morning they go down to their garage with a cup of coffee in their hand, take a look at their automotive "babies" and think, "Nice to have you here!" These customers actually don't have much time to go driving. They simply enjoy possessing things. On the other side of the coin, there are the customers who we call the "Top Guns". They have discovered their passion for driving and on Sundays, when they have time, they will go out to a racetrack to explore the limits of their vehicle. The Porsche experience also means being able to exchange thoughts within a community. That's why the community idea is such a strong part of our company. The Porsche Club is one of the oldest and largest branded clubs in the world.

Though not every customer immediately wants to become a club member.

Everyone wants to choose for themselves. However, many of our customers would like to be engaged with very beautiful and interesting things. So we invite them to panel discussions, lectures, gallery openings and other cultural events. We can offer them customised programmes.

What kind of experiences match your brand?

Since we know that a lot of our customers are interested in the arts, we have expanded our activities in cultural sponsoring. There is a partnership with the Stuttgart Ballet, which is one of the world's most renowned dance companies. The same applies to the Leipzig Gewandhaus Orchestra. We selected these two institutions because they are located in the same towns as our two main production facilities. "Made in Germany" is part of our authenticity. In addition, we are involved in sporting events, which is an obvious match for a sports car manufacturer. And then of course there are all sorts of motor racing events that lie close to the core of our brand. We initiated the Porsche Sports Cup, which has turned into one of the largest and most successful customer race series in the world. So you see, this way we are able to offer our customers and fans different experiences. These are geared to the interests of a community which, in part, money can't buy.

Owning a Porsche is still at the core of these experiences in the end though. What do you think about the idea of the "shareconomy"? Now you can even rent seats on private jets without having to own one.

We've launched some pilot projects dedicated to alternative mobility. For example, we're working with the car rental company Avis to make it possible for a particular target group to use a Porsche as a rental car. We've

> *We believe owning our product remains the*
> *most important thing. It's a testimony*
> *to this that over two-thirds of all Porsches ever*
> *built are still on the road.*

been offering this to our existing customers at selected Porsche centres for some time now. However, we believe owning our product remains the most important thing. It's a testimony to this that over two-thirds of all Porsches ever built are still on the road. This is an extremely important USP, which goes hand-in-hand with a very high retention value. After all, who wants to share their value portfolio?

CHAPTER EIGHT

SUSTAINING LUXURY

Considered consumption
and brands with substance
as the new indulgence

RETHINKING LUXURY

When LVMH announced plans in
2001 to develop its own environmental
charter and then signed onto
the United Nations Global Compact
two years later, it felt as though
someone was breaking ranks.
Until then, luxury had always put
itself above overhyped trends
and buzzwords. High-end brands did
not feel the need to participate
in the current dialogue because they
created their own dialogue. By signing
up for the UN initiative, LVMH
committed itself to adhere to
10 basic principles of human rights,
labour, environmental
protection and anti-corruption.

When LVMH began producing an annual environmental report, the move looked smart and, more than anything, the right thing to do. The company clearly saw its role as a global citizen and decided to take action. And it told everyone about it. LVMH embodies much of what we think a modern company should be: both environmentally conscious and open about its efforts.

Sustainability is here to stay. Companies are now embracing their responsibilities as global citizens and initiating change. By working to lower their environmental footprint, luxury marketers are finding support among customers. In 2012, PR house Edelman discovered that 61 per cent of consumers would opt for a brand with a good social-purpose track record when deciding between two products of equal price and quality. That is a steep jump from the low 40 percentiles in two previous annual surveys. And 63 per cent are willing to pay more for a brand that supports a good cause.

Becoming sustainable or even just shifting towards greener policies can be complex, sometimes requiring the complete revamp of manufacturing designs and supply chains. Still, demand for environmentally and labour-friendly products remains strong. Nearly half of all people surveyed in a worldwide *National Geographic* study were rated as having green consumption habits. At least a handful of luxury companies acknowledged this trend early and began adapting about a decade ago. Now, they are quite literally years ahead of the competition. Let them serve as pioneers and trailblazers and follow their lead. Ignoring the trend is perilous.

LVMH was not just a lone wolf. In 2004, Gucci began a voluntary process for social responsibility and received outside certification of its efforts three years later. In 2010, it not only introduced new fashion lines but also shipped redesigned packaging to its stores. It eliminated plastic laminated bags and paper, replacing them with recyclable materials. It has the Forest Stewardship Council certify that its paper sources are not from endangered forests and has even replaced polyester ribbons with renewable cotton. Its mannequins are made of recyclable materials. And, lately, it has been signing one environmental pact after another while releasing a string of environmentally friendly products. There are its Green Carpet Challenge handbags, which use leather from deforestation-free ranches in Brazil and are aligned with the Green Carpet charity launched by Livia Firth, the wife of actor Colin Firth. The handbags now even come with a detailed history of their donor cows' life. The company also has sunglasses made of what it calls "liquid wood" – biodegradable and supposedly composed of wood fibre, resin and lignin polymer.

Then there is its Sustainable Soles line of footwear, which basically degrades better than traditional footwear. A big part of Gucci's environmental consciousness is its two-pronged approach. It is helping to save the planet, and it is happy to let people know about it. It is difficult to read anything about sustainable luxury without running into the brand's name. If you are putting in the effort to help the planet, let your customers know. "We have done a lot but there is still a long way to go. For this reason we keep increasing our investment in terms of commitment and resources," says Rossella Ravagli, Gucci's corporate social and environmental responsibility manager.

The efforts have even flowed upwards. In 2009, Gucci parent company Kering (formerly PPR) used its deep pockets and the public's growing interest in Mother Earth for a worldwide marketing campaign that helped to increase the visibility of the luxury conglomerate and its brands while raising money for charity. The company financed showings of the film *Home*, which featured visuals of the earth and the way humans have altered it. The releases were timed with environmentally friendly product releases from Kering's many brands, including Gucci. We include this as an example of how companies can leverage green issues not only to boost environmental awareness but also to attach their brands to the issue. An infographic on page 183 illustrates Kering's environmental successes compared to its rivals. An important caveat: be sincere about your environmentally friendly intentions and actions and consumers will reward you; hide excessive emissions or labour abuses while claiming to be sustainability-conscious and you will be pilloried by consumers and the media. "Greenwashing" should not even be considered. You should be sincere about your efforts. The luxury fashion label Stella McCartney could be a role model. The successful "vegan" company does not use fur or leather for its products and tries to buy fabrics and other raw materials from sustainable sources.

The Gucci passport
Prove you are making a difference: The Green Carpet Challenge passport
certifies that the leather didn't involve deforestation.

But it also admits that it is not always possible to use sustainable products to create luxury fashion, because current supply cannot keep up with heightened demand for organic and fairtrade fabric.

SUSTAINABILITY AS BUSINESS MODEL

Consumer demand for environmentally friendly products has done more than just push industry veterans to look at their supply chains, develop green solutions and find ways to show they are doing all they can to help the environment. The demand has also created opportunities for entirely new business ideas – the environment as innovation factor – such as Livia Firth's Green Carpet Challenge, which pushes designers to incorporate sustainability into their high-end lines. Meanwhile, luxury companies should think about new product ideas, new production methods or even new business fields based on sustainability. This goes beyond concerns for the environment. Sustainable business practices also include ethical working conditions, fair-traded raw materials and long-term planning.

Loro Piana, the 200-year-old Italian cashmere producer, is enjoying strong success with a sustainable business model. The company has set up shop in Ulan Bator to monitor its wool production and make sure that it follows ethical animal husbandry rules among tribal herdsmen. Back in Italy, the company that mills the wool for use in clothes and interior furniture highlights its vertical integration as a means of controlling quality. Strictly organic? No, but deeply ethical and with a clear concern for both the environment and the bottom line. The company has leveraged a growing interest in animal welfare to support a brand image of complete excellence.

Although a complete corporate makeover as at Loro Piana is not always possible, other pioneers are creating entire companies to profit from the environmental boom. Germany's Nanai is one example. Although salmon farming itself can be controversial, using more parts of the individual salmon raised on organic farms can only be seen as a step in the right direction. Nanai takes the skins left over from salmon production and uses a vegetable-based tanning process to cure them for a variety of uses

Sustainability has long been a key component of luxury

Many companies have launched eco-activities over the past decade.

Kering committed to producing environ-mentally friendly products group-wide, and introduced a code of ethics as well as green and social audits.

LVMH launched its environmental division in 1992, and made its supply chain transparent.

Burberry conducts programmes tracking its supply chain and has joined various ethical trading initiatives.

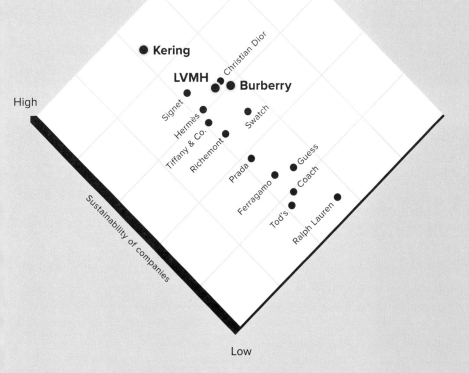

High

Low

Sustainability of companies

Kering
Christian Dior
LVMH
Burberry
Signet
Hermès
Swatch
Tiffany & Co.
Richemont
Prada
Guess
Ferragamo
Coach
Tod's
Ralph Lauren

Source: Bank Sarasin

that range from clothing to automotive interiors to furniture and even shoes. The company uses exclusively organic salmon farms and promotes the skins as a substitute for more exotic skins such as rays, snakes and crocodiles. Nanai takes its name from the Nanai people, who traditionally caught salmon in the Amur River in eastern Russia.

MADE TO LAST

To a certain extent, luxury has always been leaning towards sustainability. The entire premise of luxury is that products are made exceptionally well using the best materials. In short, luxury lasts. High-end products are the antithesis of the modern world's throwaway culture. Watches were (and are) often purchased with heirs in mind – Patek Philippe points this out in most of its marketing materials and lists "heritage", clearly defined as inheritance, as one of its 10 guiding values. Most luxury cars will be handed from one collector to the next for generations. Porsche is happy to proclaim that some 70 per cent of all the sports cars it has ever made are still on the road. A similar dynamic is at work with things like sailing yachts, jewellery and especially works of art. Reminding customers that what they are buying will be around for decades should be a cornerstone of sustainability communications for luxury companies.

BECOME TRANSPARENT

We think companies could also increase the transparency of their supply chains and manufacturing processes. If a product's materials really are the best, then let us see where they are coming from. The best of the best should always be conscious of this and, as long as no company secrets are revealed, customers should know where the tiniest part of their newest watch originated. Remember that Gucci handbag with a complete history of the cow the leather came from? That is the kind of transparency we are talking about. "People read something in *The New York Times* about how a brand doesn't produce everything in France or Italy anymore, which are the traditional countries for luxury production," says former Hugo Boss designer

Bruno Pieters, who recently launched his own Honest By brand. "They read the wallets or scarves are made somewhere else, but in terms of their perception it affects the whole brand. They think it is all made in China. It's in the interest of luxury brands to be transparent about the production of their products."

Transparency does not just have to relate to products. Companies should also be improving their business practices, aligning such things as energy use and construction to new norms with lower impact. Here, once again, companies should communicate their efforts to customers and media. These practices are not just good for public relations and marketing – they can also actually save money. "From a business perspective, our sustainability efforts not only help to build our brand equity – but save us money too," says Chuck Bennett, former VP of Earth and Community Care at Aveda. "For example, energy conservation efforts at Aveda save over $540,000 in utility costs annually. Our business has grown five times over in the past 10 years, and we're among the top five performing brands in the Estée Lauder port-folio. We are able to achieve all of this while pursuing a green agenda." Sure, Aveda is not strictly a luxury company, but it is a solid illustration of where improving business practices can lead.

CREATE NEW GREEN PRODUCTS

Along with the rise of sustainable products, a handful of sustainable luxury fairs have popped up, most notably 1.618, which each year selects distinc-tive products it feels are sustainable and then highlights them at a trade fair in Paris as well as in its online catalogue. Browsing the publication from any year shows that designers are not reinventing the wheel, they are simply turning to greener suppliers or taking environmentally friendly twists on new products, not all of which are viable yet. One of the most high profile of these companies is luxury carmaker Tesla. Its whole mission is to create electric cars without the limitations of electric cars. Tesla is fully aware that its wealthy customers are the only ones who can now afford cars in the early stage of development, where R&D is most expensive. As is visible in the 1.618 catalogues, this is becoming the norm for many areas of luxury – there are even solar gliders and yachts alongside the usual bevy of clothes made from renewable resources. Companies need not shy away from the exorbitant sticker prices of producing green products – the innovations may prove to be beneficial themselves in the way of profits. Admittedly, your company better have some experience in innovation and technology here (like a car or computer maker) but prestige and profit can come not only from consumers but also from other manufacturers.

GET CERTIFIED

Consumers today are smarter and better informed than in the past. Few are willing to simply accept the fact that your company or suppliers are working with the environment in mind just because you tell them it is so. However, sustainability has expanded beyond environmental questions to also include labour practices, not only at your company, but also at those of your suppliers. Over the past decade, corporations around the world have become accustomed to preparing sustainability reports for investors and other stakeholders, who are just as sceptical as consumers. The trend is maturing to include the provision of audited sustainability reports, much in the way corporate governance or financial statements are audited by external accounting firms or other experts. Luxury companies might want to get in the habit of not only preparing similar reports for their owners but also volunteering information on the pedigrees of supposedly green suppliers or even offering total transparency of a product's background.

This need for certification has led to an explosion in companies offering seals of approval, which may raise the question of who audits the auditors. But for now, the certification companies appear to be sparking adherence to some basic tenets of environmentalism and fair labour practices, which should be seen as positive by everyone. When looking for ways to certify green practices, companies do not have to hunt hard to find a certification agency for their particular niche. In fact, they may not have to do any searching at all – one of the world's biggest standards agencies is the best place to start for any company. The International Organisation for Standardisation is familiar to any company that ever had to introduce accountability, whether for insurance purposes, for investors or just to improve management oversight. The agency, better known as ISO, is behind the most prevalent certification system in the world. ISO has not missed the exploding interest in environment-related certification and offers an entire family of standards that we think luxury companies might want to investigate.

ISO standards are the place for any company to start its environmental certification process – first, because of the agency's deep experience in creating and establishing broad standards and, second, because certified adherence to ISO standards is such a universally recognisable signal. It simplifies the effort of communicating your company's environmentally friendly actions. ISO has developed the 14000 family of environmental standards, the basis of which is the ISO 14001:2004 certification. Admittedly, certification titles could not be less sexy, but that makes them seem all the more sincere. The 14001 certification proves your company has a viable environmental management system. The important thing is to demonstrate that your company has created and is maintaining some form of environmental management. ISO then has other standards under the 14000 heading to establish the type of labelling to reflect a company's green efforts, including reporting of greenhouse gases, specific aspects of product design and development, and environmentally friendly communications. Many luxury companies already include at least one ISO certification among their collection, underlining the necessity.

Other certifications could apply to whatever it is your company is offering. Most companies would help themselves by ensuring that any paper products (such as packaging) come from suppliers certified by the Forest Stewardship Council, which monitors forest-management practices. Tourism companies have a variety of certification opportunities, such as the Global Sustainable Tourism Council's standards or the Luxury Eco-Certification Standard from Sustainable Travel International. Restaurants can also look for certification, for example from the Marine Stewardship Council, and luxury real-estate developers and resorts can get Leadership in Energy and Environmental Design certification for construction projects. Certification agencies are easy to find but must be vetted for relevance. The same caveats should be applied

to a certification agency as to any business partner – how long they have
been in business, references and even recommendations from industry
peers. In any case, if your company is big enough, a compliance or even
environmental officer placed high up in your organisation should already
be actively looking for and applying for certifications. You do not have an
environmental or corporate social responsibility director? This could boost
the competitiveness of a company.

As stated earlier, sustainability today means more than just the environment. When consumers talk about sustainability, they also mean sustainable
work practices, not just in developed nations but also in the cheap-labour
countries. Most of today's shoppers want a clear conscience when they purchase. Luxury companies should use their wide margins to offer consumers
that clear conscience, and communicate their justification for having a clear
conscience of their own. The SA8000 standard is perfect for this. Founded
in 1997, the New York-based Social Accountability International (SAI)
has created a way to certify companies based on the way they treat their
employees as well as on how workers are treated along the supply chain.
The organisation says it bases its standards on those developed and supported by the International Labour Organisation and the United Nations.
Compliance should be simple for most luxury companies, and SAI says it
keeps an eye out for all the usual labour issues including child labour,
forced work, safety, self-determination and even management systems.

With wide margins and stratospheric expectations, there is little excuse for
luxury not to be sustainable or at least making an effort to have a smaller
environmental impact. Luxury companies should be using their prestige
and high profiles to set an example for other brands. They already offer
environmentally and socially conscious products, can easily adapt to a sustainable future, and even leverage those efforts to raise their profile and win
new customers. Sustainability is much more than a marketing strategy.

INFLUENCER
Bruno Pieters of Honest By

Being stylish and green. For a long time it was an oxymoron. Clothing made from organic materials was "good" but seldom looked great, exuding more of a muesli vibe than serious glamour. But the high-fashion industry has evolved and there has been a shift in attitude towards offering luxury that rewards not only the consumer but the producer of the garment as well.

Bruno Pieters is one of the designers pushing this movement along. And he comes with a serious pedigree, having spent much of his career working for luxury labels, among them Hugo Boss and Delvaux, Europe's oldest leather goods brand. Pieters credits a trip to India in 2011 with changing his outlook on fashion and how the garments we wear are produced. The experience affected him so profoundly that he decided to part from his own label and founded Honest By in early 2012, a brand for green fashion that is open about its production line and sold exclusively through its online store.

Vegan or organic?

Next to Pieters' designs, Honest By offers a selection of other brands such as Calla and Maison des Talons, giving each designer the opportunity to share how and where their clothes are made. The unique selling point is complete transparency, delivered visually on the website in a way not unlike any successful luxury fashion brand. Consumers can not only choose among menswear, womenswear and accessories, but are given the option to pick from vegan, organic, recycled or skin-friendly from a selection of well-made, beautiful fashion. Besides, the company only uses green energy, has a carbon-neutral delivery scheme, works with fabric that is almost exclusively certified organic, and only uses recycled paper. It is an all-round concept rather than a marketing ploy, giving the customer the chance to contribute, as 20 per cent of the company's profits are given to charity. And showing that it is after all possible simultaneously to care about things and wear fine garments.

"Explain what you do, and explain why you do it."

An interview with Barbara Coignet, founder of 1.618 Sustainable Luxury, a Paris trade fair of sustainable luxury products that highlights both new and established brands.

How did you come up with the idea of starting a trade fair about sustainable luxury?

I worked in the fashion industry for 12 years as a PR and communications liaison for designers and artists. Around 2006, I started asking my clients: Where do your products come from? Are you interested in production that is ecologically sensible? Every single one of them gave me the same answer: We can't afford to care about the environment or sustainability because we have to choose – either we are creative or we care about the planet. But I'm a curious person, and I wanted to show them that it's possible to do both. So I started looking for examples, around me, online, in other countries.

What did you find?

The easiest to identify were hotels, because they are essentially lifestyle organisations and they have to care about the environment out of necessity but also because of social aspects. When I had my proof, and kept discovering other projects around the world, I decided to showcase companies that have understood, and demonstrate that it's possible to combine creativity and sustainability. That showcase is the 1.618 fair. Sustainability is not just about ecology, it's also based on innovation and creativity. You can see it in the car companies, hotel chains, cosmetics and fashion brands that we present. Each brand has to fill out a questionnaire before they enter, judged by a committee of experts. There's a problem with greenwashing and we absolutely don't want to give a platform to brands that don't truly invest in the sustainability of their company.

Consumers from China and Brazil are only
just discovering luxury. For them,
luxury often means name, brand and power
of the brand. In those markets, they are
not so interested in questions of sustainability.

Is it mostly new brands, or do you also feature established brands?

Some brands are very new. When you are a small company with 12 people, it's easier to decide to produce sustainably compared to changing the reality of big companies. In our first year, we had brands like Sony and Tesla Motors, who were already well-known to luxury consumers. We also featured less familiar companies like Esther DuPont. The year after, BMW joined. The selection is always between 30 and 40 brands, of which perhaps 20 per cent are well-known. The rest is new.

Executives from luxury brands often argue that luxury is sustainable definition. They only work with real craftsmen, the products last a long time and so on. Do you agree?

From a philosophical standpoint – yes. The reality is often different. When a brand produces 600 bags per day, how can it say that rarity is important? True luxury companies do care and make it the focus of their commitment, and when rarity is a main concern, it coincides with a sustainable definition of luxury. But the central objective for brands is often to increase quantity. When you really want to protect the environment and your resources, you accept that resources are limited and propose high prices. That's often the difference between luxury and premium brands. Premium always wants to increase the quantity.

So the argument is true only for the very top of exclusive brands?

Resources are finite. We all know that. For true luxury companies this co-incides with their storytelling, selling rare high-quality objects. Luxury used to be the privilege of those with money and power. In the last 20 years that has changed. Today we see mass-produced accessories, by definition not luxury, sold by luxury brands. On the other hand, take Hermès. It has always based its business model on selling rarity and that hasn't changed. Hermès is an example of a luxury brand by definition and what I mean when I say that sustainability extends to social aspects. It's keeping the know-how in its own country.

But is this not the case for every luxury brand?

Not all luxury brands, which are often owned by huge companies, can be exemplary in every field. In a way, that's OK. Nobody can change everything across all aspects of a business. Both the Hermès product, which is hand-made and which you have to wait for, and the mass-produced sunglasses can be considered luxury products. They just don't derive from the same values.

H&M sells and advertises organic cotton, but most luxury boutiques don't. Does the luxury customer even care for sustainability?

We looked into that in research we conducted with HEC University in Paris. If you ask consumers whether they care about sustainability when they buy a luxury product, only 35 per cent answered that they don't care. That's a lot. More or less the same percentage, 37 per cent, answered that they do care. And the rest don't know. But what's even more interesting is that 70 per cent declared that because of its price, luxury has to respect sustainability criteria, that it would be scandalous if they didn't. So, while most consumers don't see it as an extra incentive to buy a luxury product because it is green, most of them actually expect the brand to produce sustainably in the first place.

So the topic is relevant for luxury brands?

Absolutely. Just look at what happens when there's a negative story in the press about the social aspects of a brand, or where the wood or diamonds originate from: consumers boycott the brand. And social media is an accelerating factor. Today, consumers want transparency. If they discover that a product is not sustainably produced, the brand has a huge problem. That's because customers are actually the sponsors of those companies.

The consumer still accepts paying €30,000 for a handbag.
That has remained the same. What has changed is that
they're asking questions now: Where does the leather come from?
Under which conditions was the bag made?

Are luxury brands even more vulnerable in this context than other brands?

Yes. The consumer still accepts paying €30,000 for a handbag. That has remained the same. What has changed is that they're asking questions now: Where does the leather come from? Under which conditions was the bag made? It gives them considerable power to change the market.

Gucci now sells bags with a kind of passport documenting the origins of the leather.

Gucci belongs to Kering, previously PPR, and this group has become really involved with sustainability. It always depends on the CEO or president. When he or she embraces those ideas, as Kering's François-Henri Pinault has done, they gain significance very quickly. Stella McCartney, which belongs to Kering, is a good example of a caring brand. The designer doesn't use leather or fur at all. Apparently, Kering is also planning to change the entire process and supply chain at Gucci and make the brand very green.

You said that more and more customers are asking these questions. Is this happening all over the world?

Those questions are gaining significance very quickly in Europe, which we know both because we are based there and because we issue questionnaires in stores and in partnership with HEC University each year. Every year, new issues are gaining in importance, and consumers are becoming more informed. But, of course, when we speak about luxury, we can't only speak about Europe, because the main business is generated in China today. Luxury is universal, even if brands come from Europe. Consumers from China and Brazil are only just discovering luxury. For them, luxury often means name, brand and power of the brand. They are not so interested in questions of sustainability, but that's changing more quickly than here. In China they weren't very attentive to such questions only three years ago. But now, they have the ability to address these issues, and have come to the realisation that they have to preserve their resources. So, some change is happening, and it will materialise more quickly than here in Europe.

As a consumer, if I am interested in buying sustainable, ecological products, what should I look out for when I enter a luxury shop? Should I look for certain certifications or certain labels?

Let's look at Stella McCartney as an example. The brand's labels tell the story of each product. This kind of true storytelling and transparency is important. A salesperson has to be able to answer questions about where the materials come from and where the product was made. Again, some companies are continuing to work in Bangladesh or in Turkey. They only finish the label in Italy to get the label "Made in Italy". So, if you, as a customer, buy that product, you can't be sure that it was actually entirely produced in Italy. Luxury brands have to be transparent. The problem is, the entire culture of luxury is based on being exemplary – at everything they do. They have trouble communicating that there are parts of their business that can be improved.

If you were to consult the CEO of a luxury brand, what would you recommend to him or her about this?

For fashion brands, the main issue is to increase visibility and gain control over the whole supply chain. Another issue is that, in the 21st century, you can't say, "I have to use these bad fabrics, because I don't have access to green materials". Because, actually, you do. You have the power to create them.

You also mention authentic storytelling and transparent communication about where and how the products are made.

It's quite simple. Just speak to your consumer. Look at social media. If you, as a brand, want to ask someone to be your friend on Facebook, speak to them as a friend. Explain what you do, and explain why you do it. We launched a guide where 40 brands tell their story – with video, with text, with interviews, with whatever they want – to show their consumers that their luxury car is not just a wonderful-looking product, but also what was challenging about making it. Everything will be easier when luxury brands stop being so afraid about what the media and the press will say about "greenwashing". If they're transparent, there won't be any uncomfortable questions.

CHAPTER NINE

CAPTIVATING LUXURY CONSUMERS

Creating loyal customer
relationships in a climate of declining
brand commitment

RETHINKING LUXURY

Loyalty programmes often fail –
either conceptually or in generating
a profit. This is as true for
luxury brands as it is for brands
in general. From our perspective,
the main points of discussion here are
mission, scope, the application
of knowledge about customers, staff
and expectations of technology.
It sounds easy, but luxury brands should
not underestimate the task
of moving into loyalty programmes.

But first, let's consider some context. More and more brands are trying to escape the middle- and even premium-market squeeze by approaching the luxury segment. More and more options are open to more affluent customers around the world, both physically and digitally. More and more touchpoints and technologies are available to connect with target groups. More and more loyalty programmes court customer acceptance. More and more luxury brands are operated by publicly listed companies which need to announce positive growth figures and optimistic outlooks – often diluting the brand by offering entry-level products for broader groups of less sophisticated shoppers.

Objective differences in product quality are diminishing in many categories and intangibles are becoming increasingly important for brand preference. Everybody does storytelling. And Generations Y and Z are showing less loyalty than their parents or grandparents. In addition, some particulars of the luxury market must be taken into account. Luxury lives from elitism, exclusivity, limited access for a chosen few, a strong foundation in myth (founder, owner, heritage, innovators, testimonials, materials) as much as it does from superior products and services, brand experiences or storytelling.

The idea of customer loyalty is often reduced to behaviour measured in terms of repurchase (that is, retention) and cross- or up-selling within the luxury brand portfolio. The core of standard programmes orientated around repurchase (or more-purchase) is knowing the value of individual customers. Typically, such programmes differentiate service and reward levels among A, B and C customers (gold, silver, bronze) by how much you spend. More sophisticated approaches either go for more customer groups or apply algorithms that add the customer's future value to the equation and cluster the customer base around "customer lifetime value". Developing, implementing and, especially, steadily earning money from such programmes is difficult.

"You need to be trustworthy. You need to be caring. That is very hard to do but that is the differentiator for Zappos, for the Apple stores, for Nordstrom people and for Ritz-Carlton people," says Luxury Institute CEO Milton Pedraza. "You can measure it in customer retention and you can measure it in customer referrals." Although Pedraza is talking more about premium brands, trust and caring are tickets of entry for luxury brands, too. And by bringing in customer referrals, it introduces the second dimension of loyalty: the attitudinal.

Attitudinal loyalty can even be exhibited by brand evangelists and ambassadors. And despite them being of little direct monetary value to a brand, they can be valuable multiplicators (bloggers, newsgroup administrators, community drivers) and thus affect the bottom line. While traditional loyalty programmes have been engineered around behavioural loyalty, more state-of-the art approaches also take attitudinal loyalty into account. This is driven by the rising importance of communication, interaction and communities in the digital sphere, as well as by the growing importance of mobile digital devices (smartphones, tablets) in the luxury customer's life.

LUXURY SHOPPERS AREN'T CLONES

The preconception is that luxury-brand shoppers are a relatively homogeneous target group with a somewhat traditional, Eurocentric value set. In reality there always have been significant differences between various clusters in the luxury market – old money versus new, young customers versus old, men versus women, investment versus consumption.

This is why brands as diverse as Lamborghini and Rolls-Royce, Brioni and Gucci, Bulgari and Stein, Bordeaux and Riesling wines have all prospered in their particular niches. Nowadays, the diversity is multiplying by cultures (Europe, United States, China, Latin America), marketplaces (digital and non-digital, brand-owned spaces and multi-brand spaces), affinity to technology (smartphones, tablets, 2D versus 3D), new players in the luxury market and, not least, differing privacy expectations (offering testimonials for a brand versus staying anonymous).

If one thing is obvious from the above, it is that there is no such creature as the one homogeneous luxury shopper around the globe. You cannot even trust Chinese or American or Brazilian luxury shoppers to value the same

Making them feel wanted

What matters most to today's luxury consumers.

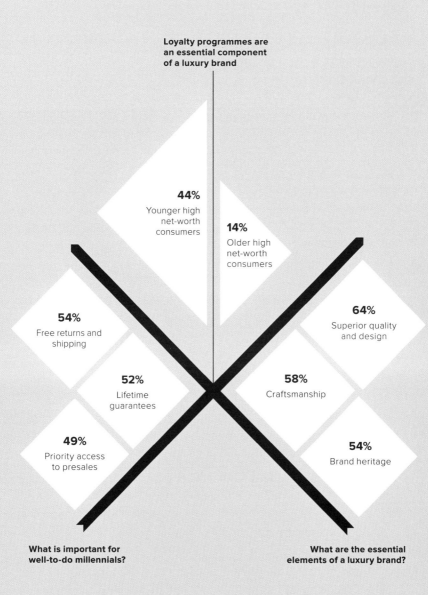

Loyalty programmes are an essential component of a luxury brand

44%
Younger high net-worth consumers

14%
Older high net-worth consumers

54%
Free returns and shipping

64%
Superior quality and design

52%
Lifetime guarantees

58%
Craftsmanship

49%
Priority access to presales

54%
Brand heritage

What is important for well-to-do millennials?

What are the essential elements of a luxury brand?

Source: Luxury Institute

things when travelling abroad that they love at home. In short, you cannot treat every brand evangelist or shopper the same way, nor should you always treat the same individual the same way. But like many other customer groups, these different and volatile luxury shoppers do have and often explicitly look for relationships with their top-end brands.

LET'S GET PERSONAL

Some decades ago, and with rather localised luxury marketplaces, craftsmen, retailers or hoteliers and concierges knew all the details of their individual customers and how to nurture loyalty from initial purchases. Especially in the bricks-and-mortar part of the business, this still holds true today. "The competitive advantage is customer culture, expressed by customer-centric human beings who out-behave the competition," says Pedraza.

Companies must ensure that their staff are their own best brand ambassadors. People on the payroll need to be big fans of the products they are selling. If they are loyal to their employer and passionate about the products or services they represent, then it will be easy and authentic to pique the interest of anyone who walks into the store.

Although premium rather than luxury, carmaker Audi is a great example. The company recently discovered it was able to boost US sales by focusing on employees, rather than customers. Audi based the dealership programme around the German word "Kundenbegeisterung", which we could translate as "inspiring customer delight". It then invited more than 10,000 dealership personnel to immersion events around the United States to teach them more about the company and how to engage with customers, and also held special workshops to reinforce the principles taught during the events. The whole thing was also wrapped up in a web-based academy for anyone who could not attend the real-time events.

The result? The company's strong US sales are supporting above-average sales growth. "Our goal was to redefine the customer experience, but first we had to win over the hearts and minds of our employees. We had to redefine the employee experience before we redefined our customer experience," says Jeri Ward, director of customer experience at Audi of America. Audi's customer loyalty in the United States has also risen more than 7 percent since 2009.

We like Audi's success here, although we know how difficult it is in times of increasing financial pressure, growing expectations of the staff and decreasing loyalty to employers to deliver consistently in this area. On the other side of the coin, one negative experience with a luxury brand's core retail staff can instantly kill a long-lasting relationship with a luxury shopper. After all, there are plenty of brand alternatives where he or she can expect to be professionally served as a valued customer. So, actively managing every member of sales staff who deals with a luxury brand or service should prove profitable.

The importance of hardware and software for managing loyalty is growing. This is driven by the global reach that luxury brands have today, the global mobility of luxury shoppers, the ubiquity of digital customer information in the 24/7 marketplaces and the ever-decreasing costs of data storage. Innumerable technical solutions, service providers, data-processing and/or analytical companies as well as loyalty process engineers and others are all trying to live from this development. But at the same time, reports of loyalty programmes that either could not be implemented or have never delivered a positive return on investment are on the increase. Why is that?

Robbie Williams once sang, "You can't manufacture a miracle". Well, you definitely can't only by applying technologies, processes and reward schemes developed for the mass or premium markets.

For the forseeable future and with most luxury shoppers, personal inter-action and the enjoyment of personalised treatment will remain vital. This is regardless of the fact that most luxury shoppers will be early adopters of the latest technologies. All the technology used for gathering, storing, analysing and deploying information about the customers of luxury brands should improve their personal brand experience rather than replace per-sonal interaction. Being human and personal in that way, companies can

Continued on page 206

Driving with friends
Bugatti offers buyers exclusive tours through northern Italy.
They are exceptional experiences which increase the bond
between participants and the brand.

Living the brand

Bugatti has its own take on luxury. The tour communicates
this by taking clients to the places in Italy where luxury lives,
creating an unforgettable experience.

create much deeper relationships with their customers and better tailor marketing activities to their particular luxury shoppers or attitudinal loyalists. Again, it is not rocket science, but at least one study shows that about half of all luxury companies do not take the time to personalise their communications. Loyal shoppers do not pay much attention to advertising and react little to a press release, but a handwritten note or invitation can provide the spark that gets them into the store. A personal touch in a hotel suite – a bottle of a customer's preferred water, chocolates or champagne in a branded wine cooler – can provide a competitive edge that a rival might have forgotten. To create loyalty, companies must show that they have been paying attention on every single occasion when they interact with their customers.

Do the bonus points and bonus miles in reward programmes satisfy this expectation of luxury customers? Or concepts that have spread to credit cards and now to special bonus retailing programmes that bundle together various chains hoping to profit from the loyalty and marketing intelligence behind the programmes? "Recognition of their loyalty through reward concepts or crediting your best customers with a higher status will encourage word-of-mouth recommendations which are hard to obtain and extremely valuable," says Richard Dixon, customer marketing director at London customer relationship consultancy Black Sun. The same is basically true for attitudinal loyalists who, for whatever reason, praise the brand without buying its products.

THE TECHNOLOGY OF LOYALTY

In the globalized 24/7 luxury brand marketplaces of today, technology is vital for distinguishing those attitudinal and/or behavioural loyalists with whom a particular brand wants to be connected from those it needs for its financial health. Additional technology is able to cluster A, B and C customers by projected customer lifetime value. Similar technology can either provide information about the service level specified for each individual customer to the staff who personally deal with them, or deliver the individualised loyalty reward directly to the customer. Different perks can be offered at different levels, whether an all-expenses paid trip to Berlin Fashion Week or the opportunity to buy tickets for an exclusive company event during Ascot. The important thing is not to offer trinkets or token gestures, but something with real value. But what is of real value differs according to culture, geography, age, gender and many other criteria. To be successful, a loyalty programme must strike a balance. A balance between being too broad to be useful for the customer (though easy for the brand owner to manage), and of being extremely individualised (but too complex to be managed profitably). With all the possibilities of scenario planning, A/B testing, real-time feedback or automated orders, only technology allows a company to walk this fine line. But at the same time it is vital to acknowledge that no technological solution will improve any kind of loyalty or provide a positive return on investment without humans...

– understanding luxury brand customer experiences and customer journeys
– understanding the business cases for individualised loyalty programmes with different service levels/reward programmes for differently valuable customers or attitudinal loyalists
– knowing about the information needed to feed the technology
– knowing about the sweet spots to be addressed or supported by the technology
– being capable of setting up a technological platform that can grow and change along with ever-changing luxury customers
– being capable of extracting the nuggets from the continuous and quite likely continuously growing stream of information.

Technology-based loyalty programmes ensure that it is not only individuals within the luxury brand who know the whims of customers, but also the company. Companies can bundle the information gathered from different areas – online and in-store, for instance – and even geographies. Who buys what, where? And who is saying or writing what about my brand? This information should then be used not only to target specific customers but also to hone marketing activities across all aspects of the customer journey. As we noted in chapter three, Chinese consumers prefer to make their first buy at home but then splurge when abroad. Companies would do well to know when the shopper who has bought from the company in Shanghai is ready to spend his or her money in London. Thus, the true benefit of technology-based loyalty programmes comes from more efficiently derived, more effectively deployed and more profitable customer satisfaction, leveraging superior customer understanding based on continuously updated data.

BIG DATA OR SMALL?

Do the chosen few attitudinal and behavioural loyalists of a luxury brand really create "big data"? Or is big data required to manage relations with luxury brand customers most profitably? Or would sensitive, high-value luxury brand customers and ambassadors really appreciate being continuously X-rayed by luxury brand owners deploying big data techniques? The amount of data gathered related to luxury brands is tiny compared to the extraordinary volumes of demographic, economic and commercial information analysed by big data companies and their software. But nevertheless, it is more than enough to help predict the lifespan and value of the relationship between loyal customers and a luxury product marketer.

Companies should rely on this information to guide their programmes. Long-term customers deserve more lavish rewards than new customers. They have given more to a company and are likely strong ambassadors. Many companies are already gathering at least some of this information. We would remind them to take advantage of it systematically, possibly leveraging the information to benefit the customer in the form of more tailored, and thus more valuable, rewards. The information should be used to create detailed profiles that permit hyper-personalised service and special offers that will help expand loyalty. If customers experience how your knowledge of them improves the tangible and intangible benefits that accompany your luxury brand, it will deepen and stabilise the relationship. We have previously mentioned the hotel that knows if a customer usually brings a dog and then has a personalised water bowl waiting in the room. This is the kind of information that should be used. That customer will stay with the hotel because they know their dog will be as well looked after. This is about caring and experiencing the feeling of being treated individually as a truly valuable customer. But does this really require big data?

A contemporary and future-proof loyalty programme should be tailored around selectively chosen information relevant for dealing with the small elite that shops in the luxury marketplace, rather than around what is typically understood as big data – broad statistical information – aimed at finding out what customers are buying and why. The latter might be an appropriate and profitable tool for mainstream or even premium brands. Everybody who has done market research with brands from these three different spheres knows how much the difficulties in recruiting and costs per interview are increased by moving from mainstream to premium to luxury, from masses to many to very few. Similarly, the costs of data generation for big data projects can exponentially increase from mass to luxury markets.

If companies opt for public rewards programmes, linking up with partners can boost their attractiveness, increase their esteem and broaden the intelligence collected. The Ritz-Carlton only recently introduced its own rewards programme and already has a network of partners that includes department stores Bergdorf Goodman and Neiman Marcus, as well as *National Geographic's* luxury tour arm. Customers can even gain points by staying at the hotels of its parent company, Marriott International. The programme has also introduced several levels of membership depending on how much customers spend – the biggest wallets obviously ascend to platinum status and points can also be spent at partner airlines. Judge for yourself whether this example from the premium brand arena can serve as a blueprint for a more sophisticated, individualised and upmarket luxury brand.

For us, more important than big data is that loyalty programmes are flexible and open enough to learn and adapt as a company discovers more about those who are spending money on its products or acting as brand ambassadors. And again, the humans dealing with (big) data or the technologies used to generate and analyse information, and using the insights they derive from it to increase luxury customer delight, are at least as important to your loyalty programme's success or failure as all the technology behind it.

LEVERAGING COMMUNITY

For both behavioural and attitudinal loyalists of luxury brands, community is essential. Even far-above-averagely powerful, affluent and influential luxury brand shoppers want to belong to a particular cohort. In addition, they need exchange with peers and brands to fuel their self-image. There are many traditional community approaches, formal or informal, that luxury brand owners can leverage. These include physical gatherings in places like Saint Tropez, Aspen, Punta del Este, Sylt or Saint Moritz; sport events such as golf tournaments, ocean races and old-timer rallies; and alumni meetings of particular schools, universities or businesses. Much of the organisation of such events has already moved into the social web – most of it in private groups, but some of it easier for luxury brand owners to access.

The social web is still a relatively young space and one that should not be ignored. Luxury companies do need to be online, as we discussed in chapter five, and to use the technology to tie customers to the brand and its image. Social web media offers companies a unique opportunity to allow their customers and passionate but attitudinal-only brand ambassadors to do some of the heavy lifting in marketing. The most controllable way is to open up and keep fuelling presences in social networks such as Facebook and Twitter, or their more elite and regional relatives across the globe.

"Controllable" means that the luxury brand owner can steer look and feel, content, access and many other aspects. Sure, anything a company posts is intensely scrutinised and targeted to convey a specific message, but the reaction can only be moderated to a certain extent. Since luxury companies create superlative products, experiences and services, the reaction does not necessarily need to be feared – as long as the company authentically, honestly, transparently and consistently lives up to its own value and the expectations raised within the customer and ambassador group.

"Fuelling" means the nurturing of this online presence with news, text, pictures and videos. Even for the vast majority of luxury brands, just providing the frame for a community means that it will develop automatically and, without continuous investment, add value to the loyalty programme or brand. Many luxury companies, including jewellery house Tiffany & Co., have had extraordinary reactions to their online efforts. Fans jump onto corporate posts to heap praise on the company and its products. This needs to be leveraged and used. Tiffany created a "True Love" campaign on Facebook that featured real photos and stories from customers. This created an emotional bond and 5 million "likes", and went a long way to bind customers. The campaign seemed to spread the message that Tiffany does not just care about its products, but also about who is using them and why. A very positive message, and much of the work was done by customers themselves. "I challenge the luxury brands to consider how to involve these types of customers as more than fans on social media. Invite them into a community that means something. Create intimacy. Reward the passion," says Jeannie Walters, chief customer experience investigator and founder of 360Connext, a Chicago customer experience consultancy.

There are exciting opportunities here for deepening and stabilising the relationship to luxury brands, while at the same time feeding the data engine of the loyalty programme and enhancing customer experience through superior knowledge. But luxury brands can do much more in the digital sphere. For example, they can provide information, audio-visual content or even products for review to bloggers, newsgroup administrators and other muliplicators. The response will usually be positive reviews and posts, usually from attitudinal ambassadors rather than customers, that further enhance a brand's fame and reach. The flip side of this approach is that the brand owner has less control and will receive less information to feed the loyalty programme. Gamification offers unique ways to connect and interact with luxury brand target groups who are living and shopping more online than offline. Here the brand owner stays more in control and benefits more from data generated. And, not least, even luxury brands can dare to sell their products and services online. Again, this is either more controllable in the brand's own online shops, providing more information for the loyalty programme. Or it is less controllable and less beneficial for the loyalty programme via third-party online stores. Many companies are already using these methods or similar technologies. But the real challenge is the smart and real-time linking of data across all the sales channels of a company. If a luxury brand wants to provide a truly seamless shopping experience, the same data should be available at every point of sale, be it online or offline, mobile or stationary. This includes a wide range of data about products, shipments, availability, regular customers and other things.

Especially with respect to online communities, there is another fine line to be walked. Luxury is built on exclusivity and restricted access for elites, while the Internet is removing barriers and democratises access. It makes sense to use web-based communities to intensify relationships with and knowledge about the chosen few customers, prospects and ambassadors, but overcome the temptation to reach out to "everybody", as this would surely dilute the brand.

CARS AND LOYALTY

Within the automotive sector, luxury cars enjoy the highest loyalty. Premium and mass-market manufacturers dream of the kind of loyalty that luxury auto brands have created. Because cars represent some of the biggest purchases made by luxury buyers, they are also some of the most infrequent. It is easier to be fickle with €4,000 handbags than with cars that cost half a million. Therefore, automotive luxury studies offer a fairly transparent view of what works and what does not. With cars, two things are vital to buyers: brand affinity and quality/reliability. Manufacturers that can offer extreme levels of quality and reliability create lifelong fans – for what would be more embarrassing than showing up at a meeting of high-end car aficionados only to have the sunroof get stuck on your latest €500,000 machine? It is also important to deliver this level of quality to brand lovers. Hell hath no fury like an enthusiast scorned. We are talking cars, but this is true for most sectors: quality and reliability are king. Interestingly, the reasons for brand loyalty differ among individual brands,

Top five factors affecting luxury automotive purchases

Luxury cars are as much about image as performance.

1.
Heritage/myth,
sponsoring,
bonding/
empathy

2.
Latest technology,
best materials,
superior
craftsmanship

3.
Power,
speed and acceleration,
superior safety
features

4.
Exclusive pricing,
brand value

5.
Unique appeal,
immediate
recognition

Source: own research

highlighting the need to know exactly why your customers like you.
Mercedes-Benz buyers, for example, love the brand's prestige but also
remain loyal because of reliability (see infographic on page 213).

This is all well and good. But there is something more here than the focus
on DQR (durability, quality, reliability) – something that makes the luxury
car buyer a different animal than the mainstream compact car buyer who
actually has to depend on his car. BMW drivers appreciate the company's
image but also want performance from their sedans. Brand and the power
of the engine certainly are among those differentiators. It was mostly for
brand reasons that Volkswagen's luxury sedan, the Phaeton, did not become the success it looked like becoming just from its undoubted quality.
Similarly, the obvious use of more reliable Ford parts has almost killed the
Jaguar brand. And looking at the power that comes in Bugattis, Bentleys,
Rolls-Royces, Ferraris, Lamborghinis – the power level delivered is in line
with the real or perceived power levels of its buyers.

Limited access to luxury cars (by numbers produced, purchase price, ser-
vicing costs) is important to demonstrate to the luxury buyer how far he is
above the crowd, how much a part of the chosen few. Heritage, myth and
visibility in the luxury shopper's peer group are key for loyalty. One important caveat regarding automotive brand loyalty is the difference between
men and women. Women remain loyal because of an exceptional dealership and service experience. This is one area where carmakers should
make conscious decisions to discover just who is doing the shopping – and
also create special buying and after-sales experiences for women. Other
businesses catering to both sexes should consider doing the same. This is
true concerning the balance between the superiority of the luxury product
and the second-best in the company's portfolio, the right service levels
granted and premiums charged.

For Bugatti this is all in sync, but for the Maybach revival that was not
the case. The product was too close to the regular Mercedes-Benz S-Class.
And the 24/7 concierge service accompanying the Maybach was not
relevant enough for the predominantly male target group, despite being
set up with high-end loyalty technology in the background and a human

(the personal concierge) delivering it to the customer. As a result, the premium charged for the Maybach was not justifiable for luxury buyers. The heritage and myth of the Maybach brand have not been strong or desirable enough to close the gap, neither for the initial purchase nor – especially – in nurturing loyalty.

CASE STUDY
Five examples of rewarding
customer loyalty

We've established that luxury consumers cannot be bundled into a homo-geneous group. But what unites them is that they like their loyalty to be acknowledged. Let us look at five ways in which luxury brands pay back their customers.

1. HON Circle

Lufthansa's elite frequent-flyer programme offers such exceptional rewards that some travellers find themselves splashing out on first-class trips or even charter jets just to maintain their status. Although HON Circle members are essentially afforded the same luxuries as the carrier's first-class passengers, they are given priority servce – the extra helping that makes the HON Circle so elite.

2. Lanvin

Limited editions are an established business model for creating a bond between customer and brand. Fashion house Lanvin has taken it a step further by producing a limited edition available only to valued customers for a specific time. A handbag made from black python leather, with a price tag of $4,000, was sold to top customers at Lanvin's Mount Street store in London. Only 14 were made – a number that says, "You, the customer, are special to us".

3. Gucci

Maybe it is no surprise that a brand known for flamboyant fashion also treats loyal customers extravagantly, offering big spenders the kind of access usu-ally reserved for celebrities. For instance, a select handful of A-list shoppers gets invitations to the menswear show in Milan with a seat in the front row and accommodation in a first-class hotel. A fitting for a custom-made suit, and private tours of the Gucci Museo in Florence and the Gucci Casellina work-shop are also included. Smaller tokens of appreciation, such as leather accessories, are dispensed throughout the trip. Gucci has also been known to invite customers to the Cannes Film Festival and equestrian events. It is a way to make the customer feel good about their spending, a "thank you" from Gucci that is also meant to encourage further spending.

4. Mr. Porter

The brother of online shopping giant Net-A-Porter carries an unparalleled selection of luxury menswear and accessories, from Balenciaga to Dolce & Gabbana to Valentino, mixed with classic sportswear and contemporary brands. Whatever the taste of the customer, and however small or large the purchase, the item arrives wrapped in black silk paper and sealed with a customised sticker bearing the customer's name. The gesture indulges the shopper's vanity and shows him that the company's appreciation does not end when the customer clicks the buy button.

"Customers want an exchange with brands."

An interview with Lutz Bethge, non-executive chairman and head of the supervisory board of Montblanc, which has successfully diversified beyond writing instruments.

Luxury brands used to know exactly who their customers were. Is this still true today?

This has changed greatly over the course of time. Going back, it was actually the nobility, in other words sovereigns, kings and princes, who invented luxury as a part of their personal lifestyle. They hired the best craftsmen of their region, country or even of the world, to create something special for them. Customers like this are no longer around. Today we see the "financial aristocracy", the ultra high net-worth individuals (UHNWs) and the high net-worth individuals (HNWIs). They are completely immune to crisis, are highly demanding and very much interested in made-to-order products and services. But of course, they are quite a small target group. Then there are the "old money" customers who have acquired a particular lifestyle over generations and are mainly conservative. At Montblanc we call them "conservative achievers". This group is somewhat larger. The luxury industry's success over the last 20 or 30 years has been to use brands to bring the luxury's elite range to the "aspirational customer". Because today, the trust we once placed in craftsmen has shifted over to brands. And the brand is hopefully authentic, and with its value, offers customers what they want.

Who do you include as aspirational customers?

This group is at least twofold. On the one hand, there are the so-called "elite of tomorrow". In the 1980s they were known as yuppies. In principle they have similar conservative thought patterns as the "old money" group. For example, a profession, career, earning money, the black Porsche as a status symbol. They want to show that they've made it. In emerging markets there are many people who fall into this first segment. Montblanc is extremely successful in the developing markets. With a product for less than €1,000, you can still symbolise a cultivated, sophisticated and successful luxury lifestyle. For other companies, this often starts at several thousand euros.

You spoke of the two groups of aspirational customers…

In mature markets such as Europe and North America, but increasingly in developing markets as well, there is a new type of "aspirational customer"

The trust we once placed in craftsmen
has shifted over to brands.
And the brand is hopefully authentic.

who advances through the story much faster. They no longer rely exclusively on the revered, traditional status symbols. Instead, they live a different lifestyle and value a work-life balance. They want to be surrounded with items that fit their lifestyle, things which are beautiful, authentic and sustainable. All of these play a bigger role, but what it finally comes down to is status. Luxury is always the aim, but status can also mean that I'm living a lifestyle that is very creative or one in which I become familiar with interesting products.

How do I get these different target groups to become loyal customers?

Authenticity is of utmost importance. This includes craftsmanship, which also needs to be represented. In 1997, when Montblanc entered into making watches, we chose the path of taking on the production process ourselves. We made a conscious decision back then to build a manufacturing facility in Switzerland, and to produce watches where the expertise and experience has been present for generations. It was a signal to customers that we mean business.

Don't new Montblanc product categories carry a danger of diluting the brand and irritating loyal customers?

When we develop products, it's important to us that they're new, modern and creative, but the customer should still love that product in 10 or 20 years' time. On the one hand there is fashion, a short-term pleasure which is popular and important to everyone. But then there are things that have a companion quality. That's what we produce. This quality must not only be reflected in longevity. The desirability of a product must also be maintained over many years. For example, my writing instrument is a

Montblanc pen that I received 24 years ago before I came to the company. It was a gift from my girlfriend at the time. She is now my wife, by the way.

The message of authenticity and timelessness – is this told the same way in all markets?

The core message, yes, but sometimes it takes on different forms. For example, we entered China in the mid-1990s. And right from the start, exclusively with our own shops, where you could experience our brand as a whole. As a result, we created a very select distribution. We deliberately utilised mega-events as a means of communication. In a market that doesn't yet know much about a brand's story, you need to do two things. On the one hand, you explain the story because in developing markets people want to buy what's "right". But in the beginning, they don't know the story. On the other hand, we wanted to communicate that Montblanc is a major brand. We achieved this through events for up to 3,500 VIP guests. We built a Montblanc city at a film studio outside Shanghai for our 100th anniversary. There was a Montblanc mountain that you could ski down, a Montblanc tramway and a Montblanc café.

Does digital storytelling work differently?

That is certainly the case. For example, we used an Internet campaign with Wim Wenders for our watch collection that we called "The Beauty of a Second". In a short trailer on our website, Wim Wenders spoke of how everyone has the potential today to make their own films. Then he announced a competition and invited filmmakers to submit their

Today, by purchasing a luxury brand
you're buying a piece of a world.
The question now is: How attractive is this world
and how can I renew it regularly?

"most beautiful second". We received tens of thousands of entries. The "Most Beautiful Second" and the "Most Beautiful 60 Seconds" won awards, and a viral campaign went global. This was a different way to access the brand and created a much more open and playful image. This is positive because Montblanc is seen as a serious brand having a certain gravitas. I really struggled with e-commerce for many years. A complication is the fact that suddenly customers are buying on the Internet and no longer in the shops. The shops are, however, important for us in order to have a dialogue with the customer. But also because we find that products bought on the Internet and in shops tend to be different ones: a customer will, for example, buy a smaller gift online – and have it sent directly to a friend – but nevertheless continue to buy high-ticket items in a shop.

As a luxury brand, you also need to be a digital storyteller, and these stories must be authentic and verifiable, right?

At the same time, you need to have a certain amount of sustainability today, because especially during tough times, people who spend thousands of euros on a watch could be viewed ambiguously. Successful brands or successful companies must give something back to society. Examples are our activities with UNICEF, who we are helping in the fight against illiteracy, or our cultural projects, such as the Montblanc de la Culture Arts Patronage Award, which honours individuals who have distinguished themselves as modern patrons. This offers us the opportunity to present ourselves as a brand in a cultivated environment. Our most loyal customers want to keep up a strong dialogue with the brand. That's why we create experiences with our events. I've just returned from Beijing where pianist Lang Lang, chairman of the Montblanc de la Culture Foundation, played for 300 guests at a dinner and also was available for casual, interesting conversations.

By purchasing a luxury item, I'm also part of a world. Is this becoming more important or was it always like this?

I think it's become much more important. It used to be that a craftsman enriched a particular customer's world. Today, by purchasing a luxury brand you're buying a piece of a world. The question now is: How attractive

*You have to constantly be thinking of new
ways to bring people together, how to excite them
and how to reach them digitally.*

is this world and how can I renew it regularly? How can I keep finding creative new ways to say something different about the same thing? That is a fine line. You have to constantly be thinking of new ways to bring people together, how to excite them and how to reach them digitally. At some point during my time as CEO at Montblanc, I decided to set up an official Montblanc CEO Facebook page where I replied to posts from customers personally. It turned into a meeting point for satisfied and dissatisfied Montblanc customers. I find that exciting.

LUXURY RETHOUGHT

Marketing exclusivity
in an age of overabundance

RETHINKING LUXURY

In this book we have shown how
fundamental technological
and societal changes have now
reached the luxury market, a market
once insulated from external
forces by its history, traditions and
wealthy customers. Technology
is making companies, products
and services more transparent for
consumers. Today's shopper
knows exactly what item they want
to buy, where to buy it and
what their peers might think of it
before they ever make their
first live contact with a company.

We have argued that, in the past, marketers only had to cater to a handful of luxury consumer types, secure in the knowledge that they had covered every base. Today, consumers are far more varied, plugged into the always-on media cycle and with niche interests fed by hyper-personal blogs, podcasts and upstart online magazines. The luxury sector is not immune to this trend and marketers now have to blur their focus and use deep fields of data to find their target audience. "This is a much more mature market that is challenging the most conservative of the luxury brands," says Armando Branchini, executive director of Fondazione Altagamma, in our interview. "But that gives much more support and potential for growth to those companies that are the best performers in the use of digital tools."

We believe that digital offerings will have to increase as generations that grew up with iPhones and tablets begin spending more and more money, but the luxury industry should be digital veterans by then, churning out web-based marketing innovations.

We have also looked at how the world is becoming more Asian, with hundreds of millionaires minted daily in China and India. Wealthy Chinese, for example, still spend plenty of money in Europe, but signs indicate they may also soon be spending more at home, and on Chinese designers. "Unfortunately, in the past 100 years China has faded from the cultural continuum," Jiang Qiong Er, CEO of Chinese luxury brand Shang Xia, tells us. "I believe that the rise of the Chinese economy will foster craftsmanship and design, but it will take some patience."

The Internet not only offers another channel to spread brand identity and reach consumers, but also makes it easier for companies to evaluate and store the purchases, interests and wishes of their customers. "Digital communication enables sales teams to connect with people and develop long-term relationships with them both in the store and beyond," explains Milton Pedraza, CEO of The Luxury Institute, in our interview. "Sales teams can reach out to customers using their digital devices and information from customer relations systems." The key point, he says, is that this enables sales teams to become radically more efficient and productive in building long-lasting relationships with customers.

Despite our enthusiasm for the Internet, we believe that the bricks-and-mortar store will not disappear. Online sales remain just a fraction of real-world transactions, and luxury has always been about surrounding customers in an overall experience of the brand. The Internet can help create terrific multimedia and interactive brand experiences, but it is no substitute for the personal and the tactile. "Without a strong base in stationary retail where people can handle the products, luxury brands don't work," Jörg Wolle, CEO of consultancy DKSH, tells us. He adds that, "We see shops as being the place where the aura and the brand experience presents itself to customers. E-commerce simply has an additional multiplier effect."

However, marketers will now need to become more creative, both in where stores should be located and in what is offered in those stores. Private shopping apartments. Exclusive events. Sales staff that caters to customers in a way that is even more individual and sophisticated than before – all with the discreet help of digital tools. Stationary retail is not going away, but it needs to become something more than it was in the past. Luxury marketing today is all about the experience – not just in retail environments but at every touchpoint. Luxury customers have always wanted to be singled out and treated in a unique way, but now they often also want to be offered the opportunity to learn and feel something no one else has.

Not least because of the Internet, luxury consumers now also require transparency in sustainability. They know the difference between simple greenwashing and truly making a difference. "While most consumers don't see it as an extra incentive to buy a luxury product because it is green, most of them actually expect the brand to produce sustainably in the first place," says Barbara Coignet, founder of the 1.618 Sustainable Luxury trade fair, in our interview. For fashion brands especially she recommends that they "gain control over the whole supply chain" and then speak to the customer about it. "Explain what you do, and explain why you do it."

Still, important questions remain. How will brands deal with increasingly fragmented customer groups? What happens when Africa starts being as affluent as Asia? Will customers keep purchasing goods or will health, self-fulfillment and even spirituality become the future of luxury, as our final interviewee, Bernd Kolb, suggests?

While the luxury market is moving away from hedonism and into critical consumption, the challenge of winning and maintaining loyal customers gets to the heart of what we have discussed in this book. Maybe Lutz Bethge, non-executive chairman and head of the supervisory board at Montblanc, puts it best when he tells us, "Today, by purchasing a luxury brand you're buying a piece of a world. The question now is: How attractive is this world and how can I renew it regularly? How can I keep finding creative new ways to say something different about the same thing?" As a luxury marketer or manager, he says, you have to constantly think of new ideas for "how to bring people together, how to excite them and how to reach them digitally". As CEO of the brand, Bethge, a sophisticated and immaculately groomed old-school gentleman, did something rather unexpected, even bold. He set up a Montblanc CEO Facebook page and personally sat down to reply to posts from customers.

That, in a nutshell, is what we mean when we talk about rethinking luxury.

"Real luxury is not made of material."

An interview with Bernd Kolb, visionary,
founder of the Club of Marrakesh
and owner of the Riad AnaYela hotel.

You successfully started a business in the new economy and led it to the stock market and then were named a member of the board at Deutsche Telekom, responsible for innovation. So you were in the classic luxury customer target group. What did you buy back then and what criteria did you use when you purchased something?

With the career I've had, there came a point in my life when I was able to afford just about anything that I wanted as far as material things are concerned. As a customer you expect to receive very intense, joyful consumer satisfaction from all these luxury products. And I have to honestly say the promises and expectations were not fulfilled.

Could you give us a list?

It was the classic mix: house, boat, sports car, fashion items – you name it. Typical of the 1990s and the 2000s. However, for me things became disappointing relatively quickly when I discovered after three days that a luxury sports car is just a car. That's one thing. The other thing is, I quickly became sated. The moment you're able say, "I can afford anything", the question arises: What do I want to afford? With all the products I'm capable of owning, I pretty quickly came to the disappointing and unsatisfying conclusion that purchasing things didn't have a large impact upon how satisfying my life was. It was a different standard of living, but it had no effect on the actual longing that was, and is, in me. However, I believe that you can only first be the judge of that if you've gone through it once yourself. The power of seduction through the "dreams" that advertising is projecting is great, and the greed simmering inside us for glitter and trinkets is large.

> *With all the products I'm capable of owning,*
> *I pretty quickly came to the disappointing and unsatisfying*
> *conclusion that purchasing things didn't have*
> *a large impact upon how satisfying my life was.*

But there were some satisfying moments, weren't there?

Anticipation is greater than the pleasure. Actually, purchasing something is already a depressing moment. It's actually really good that you can't, for instance, drive a car straight out of the show room, but may have to wait four weeks for it, because those four weeks are the best moment of the whole process. That's where the fantasy and the illusion are still perfect. It's destroyed when they become the reality. The trap that many fall into, and myself included for a while too, is to immediately try to find the next illusion. That is to say, maybe it's not the sports car. Maybe it's the sports car collection.

Always wanting more…

… it's like an addiction. The whole thing has nothing to do with needs anyway, because luxury starts when you're buying and doing things that you really don't need. When I bought myself my first yacht, the seller congratulated me on having reached the status in life where I was now able to afford a yacht. A yacht is the ultimate thing that you don't need. You are rich in luxury when you can afford things that have a disproportionate relationship between their cost and reward. A yacht is very expensive, and in fact you use it so infrequently because its true usefulness really doesn't exist.

What happens when you realise that one more sports car isn't going to make you happy?

In my case, I felt a certain amount of emptiness in the sense that, at some point, the fun I had fulfilling the dreams of my youth eventually ended. And when you see how much effort you must invest in order to live in such luxury – when you're working 14-hour days, seven days a week, having expectations that are never met – because in the meantime I must say: Real luxury doesn't come from luxury products. The next step is to ask yourself, if that's not it, then what is it? Then we have to talk about all these issues such as true experiences and adventure, perhaps even mysticism, meaning, time, nature and love. In a representative study of new German status symbols (2013), the desire "to have time" was ranked number one by far.

But you can't market mysticism, nature and love.

Oh, I believe you can.

Do I need to be a Bernd Kolb who completely refurbished a riad in Marrakesh and turned it into one of the best hotels in the world, which is both a think tank for sustainability and place of spirituality? Or does this work if I'm Gucci, Patek Philippe or Bulgari as well?

As a good marketer, you just have to recognise the true needs – this is why luxury brands are now increasingly branching out into experiences. Armani, Bulgari and others have also developed and opened hotels in recent years in which their brand can be "experienced" at its core.

How did you do it?

I was in Marrakesh and from my own experience I said, "Wow! What an incredibly mystical place. As long as I live, I will never forget those five days I spent there." Then I bought a riad in the most labyrinthine part of the old town, where no tourists actually go, and rebuilt it using very authentic and traditional construction methods, the way it was done 200 years ago. Electric tools were prohibited. We wanted to achieve that our guests are immersed in a bygone, mystical and no longer tangible world. We then packaged it as a luxury hotel. And it was a huge success worldwide.

Luxury for people who have seen and done everything?

Exactly. Not a holiday in a shielded-off space, like in clubs, that's so old luxury. Rather, new luxury. That means not everything is clinically clean and perfect, but that guests find themselves in a dirty backstreet and at first might think: My child can't play here, that would be dangerous. But we tell them, "Come with us, we're your hosts, we'll take you back there." And then they see that their children are not going to get killed, but on the contrary, that they're having a great time kicking around knotted together shreds of plastic that you could call footballs. A lot of guests were downright shocked at first because they had imagined something

Self-actualisation is the ultimate human
need and it certainly can't be reached through
"having", but only through "being".

completely different in a luxury hotel. But almost all of them were deeply touched and grateful in the end for the dream they lived. New luxury is the experiences, the learning, travelling in the Goethean sense.

In that case, new luxury would be authenticity, surprise...

... and also learning something, to be able to tell stories afterwards and perhaps it makes you more interesting to other people. I no longer just show off my new watch at my next dinner party at home, but can also say, "You won't believe what I experienced!"

In the end, is it primarily about telling stories?

When customers in saturated markets have reached the final stage of Maslow's hierarchy of needs – Maslow sees physiological needs at the bottom and self-actualisation at the top. And this is exactly the state Seneca is describing with the phrase "money has never made anyone rich". In the luxury segment you are often speaking of a desire for "things that money can't buy". In the 1980s, you made it possible for your customers to gain access to the driver's lounge at a Formula One race because the average person is not allowed in there. "Things that money can't buy" then turned into "things that money CAN buy". Self-actualisation is the ultimate human need and it certainly can't be reached through "having", but only through "being".

How important is sustainability to the idea behind new luxury?

I have been working for years now on the issue of sustainability, but I don't like hearing that term anymore. Somehow, it has run its course. It's techno-cratic, creates pressure and has no pull. There's nothing seductive about it, it isn't cool, but at best it's useful. It is really about true quality of life, in other words, the quality of what I'm experiencing.

What would be a better name then?

I'd like to replace the term "sustainability" with "quality of life". In other words, the quality of my experiences, my being, and not about useless things that wear off with time. This isn't a criticism of the idea of sustain-ability, because that's non-negotiable. I believe that luxury brands must tell a story about quality and that the quality they promise can, over time, turn into criteria for sustainability. It's no longer sufficient to speak of "high quality" nowadays. You have to explain what you specifically mean by that, what quality actually means. So then you can tell a story with "added value", and in the end, it always has to be a story that has a sustainable truthfulness to it.

APPENDIX

SOURCES

FOREWORD

P. 9

For companies such as Burberry, Burberry website, Leverage the Franchise, www.burberryplc.com/about_burberry/our_strategy/leverage-the-franchise.

Some Gucci handbags, "Gucci releases new eco leather handbags that come with 'passports' detailing each cow's entire forest-friendly life". Olivia Fleming, Daily Mail, Mail Online, March 5, 2013, http://www.dailymail.co.uk/femail/article-2288693/Gucci-releases-new-eco-leatherhandbags-come-passports-detailing-cows-entire-forest-friendly-life.html.

The United States, World Wealth Report 2013, Capgemini, RBC Wealth Management, p. 6.

China is the fastest, World Wealth Report 2013, p. 6.

And in India, World Wealth Report 2013, p. 6.

CHAPTER ONE

P. 15

"Some people think…", Coco Chanel. BrainyQuote.com, Xplore Inc, 2013, www.brainyquote.com/quotes/quotes/c/cocochanel111195.html.

P. 16

The company's history, Patek Phillipe website, company history timeline, www.patek.com/contents/default/en/history.html.

Jean Adrien Philippe joined, Patek Phillipe website, company history timeline, www.patek.com/contents/default/en/history.html.

Think of Hermès, "Hermès International S.A. History," Funding Universe website, www.fundinguniverse.com/company-histories/hermès-international-s-a-history/.

And after having excelled, Montblanc website, Corporate, www.montblanc.com/en/flash/default.aspx#/corporate.

P. 17

Luxury is present, "Views of Wealth, a Wealth of Views: Grave Goods in Iron Age Attica", Susan Langdon, in D. Lyons and R. Westbrook, eds., Women and Property in Ancient Near Eastern and Mediterranean Societies, Center for Hellenic Studies, 2005, http://chs.harvard.edu/wa/pageR?tn=ArticleWrapper&bdc=12&mn=1792.

Luxury was present, "The Two Faces of Greece: Athens and Sparta", PBS Educational Series, PBS website, www.pbs.org/empires/thegreeks/educational/lesson1.html.

A couple of hundred years, "Lex Oppia", Encyclopedia Brittanica website, www.britannica.com/EBchecked/topic/338333/Lex-Oppia.

However, John Calvin, "What Exactly did Jean Calvin (1509–1564) do for Geneva?", Diva International website, http://divainternational.ch/spip.php?article90.

P. 18–19

Infographic: Roland Berger Strategy Consultants Vorlesung, Luxury Marketing.

P. 20

It is now widely, "John Calvin's Austerity and the Birth of the Swiss Watch Industry", Max E. Reddick, Monochrome online magazine, November 13, 2012, www.monochrome-watches.com/john-calvins-austerity-and-the-birth-of-the-swiss-watch-industry.

And, as more people, "Did living standards improve during the Industrial Revolution?", C.W. London, The Economist website, September 13, 2013, www.economist.com/blogs/freeexchange/2013/09/economic-history-0.

P. 21

In the early 19th, Hermès website, history, http://lesailes.hermes.com/us/en/.

Three big luxury, "Taking Stock: An Inventory of Consolidation in the Luxury Industry", Sophie Doran, Luxury Society website, September 27, 2013, http://luxurysociety.com/articles/2013/09/taking-stock-an-inventory-of-consolidation-in-the-luxury-industry.

LVMH also owns, LVMH website, LVMH companies and brands, www.lvmh.com/the-group/lvmh-companies-and-brands.

Richemont sells, Richemont website, our businesses, www.richemont.com/our-businesses.html.

Kering has, Kering website, brands, www.kering.com/en/brands.

But in the 1990s, "The 1990–91 Recession in Historical Perspective", Stephen K. McNees, New England Economic Review, January/February 1992, www.bostonfed.org/economic/neer/neer1992/neer192a.pdf.

P. 23

In the past 15, 2012 Luxury Goods Worldwide Market Study (11th Edition), Altagamma Foundation, Bain & Company, p. 4.

The market stalled, 2012 Luxury Goods Worldwide Market Study (11th Edition), p. 4.

After catching its, 2012 Luxury Goods Worldwide Market Study (11th Edition), p. 4.

It contracted, 2012 Luxury Goods Worldwide Market Study (11th Edition), p. 4.

That market is worth, 2012 Luxury Goods Worldwide Market Study (11th Edition), p. 2.

Folding in those items, 2012 Luxury Goods Worldwide Market Study (11th Edition), p. 2.

And the overall, 2012 Luxury Goods Worldwide Market Study (11th Edition), p. 15.

Fresh millionaires, "China produces fewer millionaires as economy slows", Agence France-Presse in Shanghai, South China Morning Post website, August 15, 2013, www.scmp.com/news/china/article/1296886/china-produces-fewer-millionaires-economy-slows.

P. 24

The United States remains, 2012 Luxury Goods Worldwide Market Study (11th Edition), p. 2.

Brazil is home, Worldwide Luxury Markets Monitor Spring 2013 Update, Altagamma Foundation, Bain & Company, p. 8.

Indian customers, "Luxury marketing in India: The Indian Touch", Glyn Atwal, Branding Magazine website, October 15, 2012, www.brandingmagazine.com/2012/10/15/luxury-marketing-india/.

America's luxury market, 2013 Luxury Goods Worldwide Market Study (12th Edition), October 2013, pp. 14 & 16.

Europe is a popular, 2013 Luxury Goods Worldwide Market Study (12th Edition), October 2013, Altagamma Foundation, Bain & Company, p. 15.

Using a yardstick, "Roland Berger Study On The Luxury Goods Market: Germany Has The Biggest Potential In Europe", Roland Berger website press release, April 16, 2012, http://www.rolandberger.com/media/press_releases/512-press archive2012_sc_content/Roland_Berger_study_on_luxury_goods_market.html.

France and Italy, "Roland Berger Study On The Luxury Goods Market: Germany Has The Biggest Potential In Europe", Roland Berger website press release, April 16, 2012.

It is not surprising, Worldwide Luxury Markets Monitor Spring 2013 Update, p. 12.

Coupled with, Worldwide Luxury Markets Monitor Spring 2013 Update, p. 12.

Despite recent problems, Worldwide Luxury Markets Monitor Spring 2013 Update, p. 8.

Japan is Asia's, Worldwide Luxury Markets Monitor Spring 2013 Update, pp. 9 & 11.

P. 27

This Ming vase, BBC News, "Chinese Ming vase smashes auction record in Hong Kong", BBC News website, October 5, 2011, www.bbc.co.uk/news/world-asia-pacific-15180781.

P. 28

Hans Waldmann, Encyclopædia Britannica website, 2013, www.britannica.com/EBchecked/topic/634438/Hans-Waldmann.

P. 30

Harpsichord, Music for the Harpsichord, Victoria and Albert Museum website, http://www.vam.ac.uk/content/articles/m/music-for-the-harpsichord/.

P. 31

Thierry Hermès, Hermès website, history, http://lesailes.hermes.com/us/en/.

P. 32

Patek Philippe, Patek Philippe website, http://www.patek.com.

P. 33

This Bentley, "Birkin Blower", "1929 Blower Bentley – Auto Shows" Road & Track website, John Lamm, April 29, 2011, www.roadandtrack.com/car-shows/art-of-the-automobile/1929-blower-bentley.

P. 34

Bernard Arnault, LVMH website, executive committee, www.lvmh.com investor-relations/lvmh-at-a-glance/executive-committee/bernard-arnault.

CHAPTER TWO

P. 45

However, only small, "2. Kunden- und Produktstrategien" (in German), Philip Beil, Martin C. Wittig, Roland Berger/Uni St. Gallen Luxusmarketing Wintersemester 2012/2013.

P. 46

We are also seeing, "2011 – Der deutsche Luxusmarkt wächst Rasant" (in German), Roland Berger Strategy Consultants, Meisterkreis – Deutsches Forum für Luxus, market study, April 12, 2012, www.rolandberger.com/media/pdf/Roland_Berger_Luxusstudie_D_20120416.pdf.

P. 52

Most buyers of luxury, "Luxury Goods in the US", Euromonitor Country Report, website summary, January 2013, www.euromonitor.com/luxury-goods-in-the-us/report.

Among the affluent, Richistan, Robert Frank, Three Rivers Press, 2007, p. 124.

P. 53

The demand for, 2012 Luxury Goods Worldwide Market Study (11th Edition), p. 36.

Another specific, 2013 Luxury Goods Worldwide Market Study (12th Edition), p. 29.

Russians are the world's, "2012 was outstanding year for Global Blue Tax Free Shopping", Global Blue website, 2012, http://business.globalblue.com/news-archive/2012-was-outstanding-year-for-global-blue-tax-free-shopping/.

P. 53 & 54

A new generation, Russian Millionaires: A New Generation, Dr Natalia Tikhonova, Ria Novosti, May 26, 2004, http://en.ria.ru/analysis/20040526/39917064.html.

P. 54

Luxury consumers in the Emirates focus, Eyewear in the United Arab Emirates Country Report, Euromonitor International, December 2012, www.euromonitor.com/eyewear-in-the-united-arab-emirates/report.

P. 54

Although an estimated, World Development Indicators India, The World Bank, 2013, http://povertydata.worldbank.org/poverty/country/IND.

Dollar millionaires increased, World Wealth Report 2013, Capgemini and RBC Wealth Management, 2013, p.6, www.capgemini.com/sites/default/files/resource/pdf/wwr_2013_0.pdf.

Only Hong Kong, World Wealth Report 2013, Capgemini and RBC Wealth Management, 2013, p.6, www.capgemini.com/sites/default/files/resource/pdf/wwr_2013_0.pdf.

Still, the luxury, "Big Brand Theories", Debashish Mukerji, Business Today website, September 1, 2013, http://businesstoday.intoday.in/story/indian-luxury-market-book-authors-share-trends/1/197656.html.

As a result, the sales, 2012 Luxury Goods Worldwide Market Study (11th Edition), p. 16.

And since import taxes, "How Much Customs Duty You Have to Pay for Importing Goods into India", Amit Agarwal, Digital Inspiration Website, May 30, 2013, http://www.labnol.org/india/custom-import-duties/.

CHAPTER THREE

P. 66

Peng Liyuan is collecting, "Peng Liyuan: the 'Kate Middleton' effect of China's new first lady", Malcolm Moore, Daily Telegraph website, Malcolm Moore, March 24, 2013, www.telegraph.co.uk/news/worldnews/asia/china/9951016/Peng-Liyuan-the-Kate-Middleton-effect-of-Chinas-new-first-lady.html.

P. 67

The ascension of China, "Hermès tests European appetite for its young Chinese brand", Astrid Wendlandt, Pascale Denis, Reuters, September 11, 2013, www.reuters.com/article/2013/09/11/us-hermes-shangxia-idUSBRE98A11X20130911.

In 2012, the Chinese, 2012 Luxury Goods Worldwide Market Study (11th Edition), p. 2.

Wealthy Chinese from, Worldwide Luxury Goods Monitor Spring Update, 2013, p. 11.

The country is only, World Population Data Sheet 2012, Population Reference Bureau, Washington DC, www.prb.org/Publications/Datasheets/2012/world population-data-sheet/data-sheet.aspx.
&
"China produces fewer millionaires as economy slows", Agence France-Presse in Shanghai, South China Morning Post website, August 15, 2013, www.scmp.com/news/china/article/1296886/china-produces-fewer-millionaires economy-slows.

The brand, Shang Xia, Shang Xia website, www.shang-xia.com/en/artistic-director.

"I believe that…", Taken from the interview conducted with Jiang Qiong Er.

P. 68

In 2005, Japan, Roland Berger Strategy Consultants Vorlesung, Luxury Marketing.

Just seven years, Roland Berger Strategy Consultants Vorlesung, Luxury Marketing.

Although China lags Germany, Credit Suisse Global Wealth Report 2012,
Giles Keating, Michael O'Sullivan, Anthony Shorrocks, James B. Davies,
Rodrigo Lluberas, Antonios Koutsoukis, Credit Suisse, October 2012, p. 21.

The Chinese are transitioning, 2013 Luxury Goods Worldwide Market Study (12th Edition),
pp. 18 & 31

P. 69

We discovered that, Roland Berger Strategy Consultants Vorlesung, Luxury Marketing, slide 29.

We also found, Roland Berger Strategy Consultants Vorlesung, Luxury Marketing Asia, slide 29.

And, above them, Roland Berger Strategy Consultants Vorlesung, Luxury Marketing Asia, slide 29.

"What they're going…", "A Creator Of Hulu Is Teaming Up With Yahoo's Ex-CEO To Take On
The China Market", Owen Thomas, Business Insider website, July 18, 2012,
www.businessinsider.com/brian-buchwald-terry-semel-bomoda-2012-7.

Chinese consumers prefer, "Understanding social media in China",
Cindy Chiu, Chris Ip, Ari Silverman, McKinsey Quarterly, April 2012.

The top three, The World luxury Index™ China 2013: The Most Sought-After
Luxury Brands, Digital Luxury Group, Luxury Society, June 27, 2013,
www.digital-luxury.com/#!/2013/06/the-world-luxury-index-china-2013-the-
most-sought-after-luxury-brands/.

Initial purchases of a specific brand, 2013 Luxury Goods Worldwide Market Study
(12th Edition), p. 17.

P. 69 & 71

Heavyweights such as, Hermès website: http://stores.hermes.com/Asia/China/Beijing/
Hermes-China-World. Gucci website: www.gucci.com/cn-en/storelocator.

P. 70

Infographic: 2013 Luxury Goods Worldwide Market Study (12th Edition), pp. 9 & 11.

P. 71

When looking at China, "Luxury brands still reaping big rewards in China", Ernest Kao,
South China Morning Post website, February 18, 2013, www.scmp.com/news/china/
article/1153131/luxury-brands-still-reaping-big-margins-china-market.
&
"China Rethinks Luxe Tariff Proposal to Reduce Import Duties on High-End Goods
Faces Political Hurdles", Laurie Burkitt, Wall Street Journal website, June 29, 2011,
http://online.wsj.com/news/articles/SB100014240527023036271045764134006602
67500.

Although the government, "Exporters Ready to Milk Chinese Tariff Cuts",
Scott Murdoch, The Australian website, December 20, 2012,
www.theaustralian.com.au/business/exporters-ready-to-milk-chinese-tariff-cuts/
story-e6frg8zx-1226540704397#.

Only a small, "Luxury Without Borders: China's New Class of Shoppers Take on
the World", Yuval Atsmon, Diane Ducarme, Max Magni, Cathy Wu, McKinsey
Consumer Survey, December 4, 2012, Exhibit 4: p. 21.

However, about half, "Luxury Without Borders: China's New Class of Shoppers
Take on the World", McKinsey Consumer Survey, p. 21.

Although technically the Chinese, 2013 Luxury Goods Worldwide Market Study
(12th Edition), pp. 18 & 20.

P. 72

Some analysts believe, "Mainland Chinese tourists help push up sales at Prada", Anita Lam,
South China Morning Post website, Feb. 20, 2013, www.scmp.com/business/companies/
article/1154253/mainland-chinese-tourists-help-push-sales-prada.

That buying, "Mainland Chinese tourists help push up sales at Prada", Anita Lam, South China Morning Post website, February 20, 2013, www.scmp.com/business/companies/article/1154253/mainland-chinese-tourists-help-push-sales-prada.

Places such as Singapore, "Korean Luxury Retailers See Surge In Chinese Tourist Spending", Jing Daily, Jing Daily website, August 24, 2012, www.jingdaily.com/korean-luxury-retailers-see-surge-in-chinese-tourist-spending/20407/.

The intrusion of, "With Psy and currency swaps, South Korea grabs global influence", Se Young Lee, Christine Kim, Reuters website, October 21, 2013, www.reuters.com/article/2013/10/21/us-korea-economy-diplomacy-idUSBRE99K11U20131021.
&
"South Korea eases visa rules to attract more Chinese tourists", Audrey Yoo, South China Morning Post website, August 12, 2013, www.scmp.com/news/china-insider/article/1296120/south-korea-eases-visa-rules-attract-more-chinese-tourists.

In late 2012, "PPR Aims to Buy More Chinese Brands After Acquiring Qeelin", Andrew Roberts, Vinicy Chan, Bloomberg.com, December 10, 2012, www.bloomberg.com/news/2012-12-09/ppr-acquires-chinese-jeweler-qeelin-for-undisclosed-price.html.

It did not say, "PPR Aims to Buy More Chinese Brands After Acquiring Qeelin", Andrew Roberts, Vinicy Chan, Bloomberg.com, December 10, 2012.

Its jewellery, "PPR Aims to Buy More Chinese Brands After Acquiring Qeelin", Andrew Roberts, Vinicy Chan, Bloomberg.com, December 10, 2012.

After a leadership, "China gift crackdown hits watches, booze but foreign brands hold on", Adam Jourdan, Reuters website, January 15, 2013, www.reuters.com/article/2013/01/15/china-luxury-gifts-idUSL4N0AK2B820130115.

P. 73
infographic: 2012 Luxury Goods Worldwide Market Study (11th Edition), p. 28.

P. 72 & 74
While the anti-corruption, "Gift-Giving Crackdown Hits China Luxury Retailers", Katie Holliday, CNBC website, February 8, 2013, www.cnbc.com/id/100445071.

P. 74
Officials have said, "Gift-Giving Crackdown Hits China Luxury Retailers", Katie Holliday, CNBC website, February 8, 2013, www.cnbc.com/id/100445071.

The ads, it said, "China bans ads for pricey gifts in anti-corruption push", Robert Birsel, Reuters website, February 6, 2013, http://uk.reuters.com article/2013/02/06/uk-china-tv-corruption-idUKBRE91505620130206.

It began blossoming, "Japan's luxury shoppers move on", Brian S. Salsberg, McKinsey & Company, August 2009, www.mckinsey.com/insights/consumer_and_retail/japans_luxury_shoppers_move_on.

Currently the world's third-largest, "Consumer in 2050 – The rise of the EM middle class", HSBC Global Research, Karen Ward, Frederic Neumann, October 2012, p. 29, www.hsbc.com.vn/1/PA_ES_Content_Mgmt/content/vietnam/abouthsbc/newsroom/attached_files/HSBC_report_Consumer_in_2050_EN.pdf.

Burberry, along; "Japan's luxury shoppers move on", Brian S. Salsberg, McKinsey & Company, August 2009.

P. 74 & 75
Japanese customers account, "Deluxe: How Luxury Lost Its Luster", Dana Thomas, Penguin Press HC, 2007.
&
"The Devil Wears Hermès (He Bought It at the Caesars Palace Mall in Las Vegas)",

Michiko Kakutani, New York Times website, August 21, 2007,
www.nytimes.com/2007/08/21/books/21kaku.html.
&
LVMH Interim Financial Report Six-Month Period Ended June 30, 2013, p. 11.

P. 75

Gucci built not just, Gucci website, www.gucci.com/us/worldofgucci/articles/japan-flagship.

Cosmetics company Shiseido, Shiseido website, parlour.shiseido.co.jp/ginza/e/index.html.

Versace abandoned the market, "Versace quits Japan after 30 years", Michiyo Nakamoto,
The Financial Times website, October 7, 2009, www.ft.com/intl/cms/s/0/e5e6a886-b325-
11de-ac13-00144feab49a.html#axzz2gZe00O6s.
&
Versace website (list of shops in Japan, 2013), www.versace.com/en/find-a-boutique/Japan.

P. 78

Japan's modern luxury consumers, 2013 Luxury Goods Worldwide Market Study (12th Edition),
October 2013, Altagamma Foundation, Bain & Company, p. 16.

Burberry Black Label and Blue Label, "Burberry Blue Label – Tokyo, Japan", 2007,
Kineda website, www.kineda.com/burberry-blue-label-tokyo-japan/.
&
"Burberry Black Label – Tokyo, Japan", 2007, Kineda website,
www.kineda.com/burberry-black-label-tokyo-japan/.

Arguments can be made, "Lanvin en Bleu Designer Bio", Styleon.com,
http://styledon.com/brands/lanvin-en-bleu#.
Lanvin Collection website, www.joix-corp.com/lanvin/.

Outlet malls are a common sight, "Outlet malls another American concept that may not
work in Japan", Philip Brasor, Masako Tsubuku, The Japan Times website, April 16, 2012,
http://blog.japantimes.co.jp/yen-for-living/outlet-malls-another-american-concept-that-
may-not-work-in-japan/.

Another Asian luxury market we note, Worldwide Luxury Markets Monitor Spring 2013 Update, p. 11.

P. 79

Even tourism is booming, "Foreign Tourists to South Korea Already Number Ten Million
This Year", November 27, 2013, Business Korea website, www.businesskorea.co.kr/
article/2293/tourism-korea-foreign-tourists-south-korea-already-number-ten-million-year.

Luxury Hall West, "Where to Shop", Korea Tourism Organisation website,
http://english.visitkorea.or.kr/enu/SH/SH_EN_7_2.jsp?cid=273773.

One reason is, Annual Labour Force Statistics, OECD website, http://stats.oecd.org/
Index.aspx?DataSetCode=ANHRS.
&
"Korea's Luxury Market: Demanding Consumers but Room to Grow", Aimee Kim
and Martine Shin, McKinsey & Company, Consumer and Shopper Insights August 2011, p. 1.

"There is a remarkable…", "S Korea luxury: beyond the obvious", Christian Oliver,
Financial Times website, September 13, 2011, http://blogs.ft.com/beyond-brics/2011/09/13/
luxury-in-s-korea-look-beyond-the-obvious/#axzz2mEbQNHZe.

P. 80

Research into the buying habits, "Luxury Without Borders: China's New Class of Shoppers
Take on the World", McKinsey Consumer Survey, p.27.

Thecorner.cn, Yoox Group, thecorner.com, www.yooxgroup.com/en/thecorner.asp.

P. 81

It was only in 2010, "Emporio Armani Launches Online Store in China", Luisa Zargani, WWD, November, 25 2010, www.wwd.com/retail-news/designer-luxury/emporio-armani-launches-online-store-in-china-3390940.

But since then, "Luxury Without Borders: China's New Class of Shoppers Take on the World", McKinsey Consumer Survey, p.27.
&
2013 Luxury Goods Worldwide Market Study (12th Edition), October 2013, p. 18.
&
2012 Luxury Goods Worldwide Market Study (11th Edition), October 2012, p. 17.

In February 2013, "China's 360Buy picks up $400m Series D funding led by Twitter investor Alwaleed bin Talal", Josh Ong, The Next Web website, February 18, 2013, http://thenextweb.com/asia/2013/02/18/chinas-360buy-picks-up-400m-investment-led-by-saudi-prince-alwaleed-bin-talal/.

Because here is another number, "Chinese e-luxury market to grow to RMB 45.3 billion by 2015", Noor Fathima Warsia Digital Market Asia, June 28, 2013, www.digitalmarket.asia/2013/06/chinese-e-luxury-market-to-grow-to-rmb-45-3-bln-by-2015/.

Social media, "The Importance of Social Media in China", Simon O'Connell, Global Blue website, 2012, www.globalblue.com/corporate/news/the-importance-of-social-media-in-china/.

The country often, "Want To Capitalize On China? You Better Have Good Guanxi", Languatica (Christopher Warren-Gash), Forbes website, March 15, 2012, www.forbes.com/sites/languatica/2012/03/15/want-to-capitalize-on-china-you-better-have-good-guanxi/.

RenRen appeals to those in their twenties, while Sina Weibo reaches people firmly in their careers, "Sina Weibo", Gady Epstein, Forbes website, March 3, 2011, www.forbes.com/global/2011/0314/features-charles-chao-twitter-fanfou-china-sina-weibo.html.

CHAPTER FOUR

P. 90

Patrick-Louis Vuitton, "Patrick Louis Vuitton im WOMAN-Interview" (in German), Woman, Clara Bilek, November 26, 2012, www.woman.at/a/patrick-louis-vuitton-woman-interview-347232.

P. 91

"There will always…", "Die Ära des Jetset ist vorbei" (in German), Thomas Bärnthaler, Süddeutsche Zeitung Magazin, Heft 16 2013, http://sz-magazin.sueddeutsche.de/texte/anzeigen/39827.

"But business travellers…", "Die Ära des Jetset ist vorbei", Thomas Bärnthaler.

"Among the customers…", "Die Ära des Jetset ist vorbei", Thomas Bärnthaler.

Vuitton receives, "Patrick Louis Vuitton im WOMAN-Interview", Clara Bilek.

Men like, "John Thain's $87,000 Rug", Charlie Gasparino, The Daily Beast, January 22, 2009, www.thedailybeast.com/articles/2009/01/22/john-thains-87000-rug.html.

P. 91 & 92

Or the executives of Citigroup, "Citi Reverses Course on $50 Million Jet", Cyrus Sanati, Dealbook/New York Times, January 27, 2009, http://dealbook.nytimes.com/2009/01/27/citi-reverses-course-on-50-million-jet/?_r=0.

P. 92

This habit of, The Theory of the Leisure Class: An Economic Study of Institutions, Thorstein Veblen, New York, The Macmillan Company, 1915 edition, p. 68.

Veblen wrote, The Theory of the Leisure Class: An Economic Study of Institutions, Thorstein Veblen, p. 103.

According to Veblen, The Theory of the Leisure Class: An Economic Study of Institutions, Thorstein Veblen, p. 103.

P. 93

In his 2000 book, Bobos in Paradise, Bobos in Paradise: The New Upper Class and How They Got There, David Brooks, Simon and Schuster, 2000.

Brooks writes, Bobos in Paradise: The New Upper Class and How They Got There, David Brooks, p. 84.

Furthermore, "The members . . . ", Bobos in Paradise: The New Upper Class and How They Got There, David Brooks, p. 85.

P. 94

Of those questioned, Roland Berger Vorlesung Luxusmarketing (in German), 2012/2013, September 17, 2012, University St. Gallen, Martin C. Wittig, p. 7.

Yet 87 percent, Roland Berger Vorlesung Luxusmarketing, 2012/2013, p. 7.

The famous Hermès scarf, "Portrait of the Artist as a Postman", Texas Monthly, Jason Sheeler, October 2012, www.texasmonthly.com/story/portrait-artist-postman.
Some of the most popular, "Portrait of the Artist as a Postman", Jason Sheeler.

P. 94 & 95

Kermit Oliver, "Portrait of the Artist as a Postman", Jason Sheeler.

P. 95

Women like Jackie Onassis, "Portrait of the Artist as a Postman", Jason Sheeler.

Under the banner, Manufactum website, www.manufactum.com/home.html.

At Manufactum, Manufactum website, http://www.manufactum.de.

Or the Danish, Manufactum website, http://www.manufactum.de.

Manufactum also has reeditioned, Manufactum website, http://www.manufactum.de.

Anderson & Sheppard, Anderson & Sheppard website, www.anderson-sheppard.co.uk.

P. 95 & 97

"You never actually own. . .", Patek Phillipe website, 2013, www.patek.com/contents/default/en/advertising2013.html.

P. 97

In another ad, Patek Phillipe website, "Meeting Up", 2013, www.patek.com/contents/default/en/advertising2013.html.

In 2012, two-thirds, "Luxury Without Borders: China's New Class of Shoppers Take on the World", p. 25.

In 2010, "Luxury Without Borders: China's New Class of Shoppers Take on the World", p. 25 .

Similarly, more than one-half, "Luxury Without Borders: China's New Class of Shoppers Take on the World", p. 24 .

This is now equal to, "Luxury Without Borders: China's New Class of Shoppers Take on the World", p. 24.

P. 98

Infographic: World Bank.

As an expert of, Mary Egan, quoted in: "The Luxury Market: Trying to Hit a Moving Target", Wharton, March 30, 2005, http://knowledge.wharton.upenn.edu/article/the-luxury-market-trying-to-hit-a-moving-target/.

P. 99

Limited editions, "Dries Van Noten Will Let You Design Your Own Dress", Susannah Edelbaum, Under Retail Trends, The High Low, July 14, 2011, http://thehighlow.com/2011/07/dries-van-noten-will-let-you-design-your-own-dress/.
&
"Montblanc On How To Be A Luxury Brand For Many", Ariel Adams, Forbes, March 14, 2013, www.forbes.com/sites/arieladams/2013/03/14/montblanc-on-how-to-be-a-luxury-brand-for-many/.

But the person, "The Row's $39,000 Alligator Backpack Sold Out", Ellie Krupnick, The Huffington Post, October 3, 2011, www.huffingtonpost.com/2011/10/03/the-row-backpack-sold-out_n_992606.html.

The Row's backpack, The Row's $39,000 Alligator Backpack Sold Out", Ellie Krupnick.

P. 100

But many were surprised, "The fall and rise of Victoria Beckham, fashion designer", Ellis Cashmere, Staffordshire University blog, October 16, 2013, http://blogs.staffs.ac.uk/elliscashmore/2013/10/16/the-fall-and-rise-of-victoria-beckham-fashion-designer/.

The locations are understated, Victoria Beckham website, www.victoriabeckham.com/store-locator.

Her first London outlet, "Victoria Beckham set to open her own clothing store in London's Mayfair", Kirsty McCormack, Daily Express website October 14, 2013, www.express.co.uk/news/showbiz/436681/Victoria-Beckham-set-to-open-her-own-clothing-store-in-London-s-Mayfair.

Beckham said, "Victoria Beckham Launches Mainline Online", Lauren Milligan, Vogue, September 27, 2013, www.vogue.co.uk/news/2013/09/27/victoria-beckham-mainline-launching-on-Website.

The brand's success, "The Power List 2013", BBC Radio 4 website, www.bbc.co.uk/programmes/b007qlvb/features/power-list-100.

CHAPTER FIVE

P. 110

The Internet changed everything, Taken from the video series "Pardon My French", episode "Meeting Dries Van Noten", Garance Doré, April 4, 2013, www.garancedore.fr/en/2013/04/04/pardon-my-french-dries-van-noten/.

P. 111

Dries Van Noten's open-mindedness, The Fashion Trail – Alma Mater of the Antwerp Six Celebrates, Eugene Rabkin, The Business of Fashion, September 9, 2013, www.businessoffashion.com/2013/09/antwerp-royal-academy-ann-demeulemeester-dries-van-noten-dirk-bikkimbergs-walter-van-beirendonck.html.

Global online sales of luxury goods, 2012 Luxury Goods Worldwide Market Study (11th Edition), p. 10.

P. 112

Generation X and Y shoppers, "Meet The Millennial 1%: Young, Rich, And Redefining Luxury", Forbes website, Larissa Faw, February 10, 2012, www.forbes.com/sites/larissafaw/2012/10/02/meet-the-millennial-1-young-rich-and-redefining-luxury/.

Research indicates that they are, "Meet The Millennial 1%: Young, Rich, And Redefining Luxury", Larissa Faw.

Research among affluent consumers, "Introducing Putting the Luxe Back in Luxury", (Pamela N. Danziger, Putting the Luxe Back in Luxury, 2011), Unity Marketing Online, December 14, 2012, www.unitymarketingonline.com/cms/Home/Luxury_Press_Releases/12-14-2012_Affluents Online_Intro.php.

Interestingly, nearly half, "Introducing Putting the Luxe Back in Luxury", (Pamela N. Danziger, Putting the Luxe Back in Luxury), Unity Marketing Online.

Some 2.4 billion PCs, laptops, Gartner Market Research, April 2013, www.gartner.com/newsroom/id/2408515.

P. 113:

Vacheron Constantin, Vacheron Constantin, The Hour Lounge website, www.thehourlounge.com/index.php?module=Thread&action=listAll.

Research suggests that wealthy shoppers, "Luxus im Netz", TextilWirtschaft, Sabine Spieler, Ausgabe 14, April 7, 2011, www.textilwirtschaft.de.

Another study found, "72pc affluent consumers have no spending limit in apps: study", by Rachel Lamb, Luxury Daily website, April 25, 2012, www.luxurydaily.com/affluent-consumers-favor-brands-with-apps-study/.

P. 114:

Jaeger-LeCoultre, Jaeger-LeCoultre website: News, November 25, 2010, www.jaeger-lecoultre.com/WW/en/content/the-jaeger-lecoultre-iphone-application-rewarded.html.

P. 115:

Girard-Perregaux, "Girard-Perregaux Releases iPhone and iPad App", Mike Disher WatchTime.com, November 16, 2010, www.watchtime.com/wristwatch-industry-news/technology/girard-perregaux-releases-iphone-and-ipad-app/#.

Linde Werdelin, Linde Werdelin website, "Another New Year, Another New Season", posted on January 21, 2010, www.lindewerdelin.com/thelab/another-new-year-another-new-season.

P. 116:

Net-A-Porter, "Natalie Massenet sells Net-a-Porter stake to Richemont for £50m", Alexandra Topping, The Guardian website, April 1, 2010, www.theguardian.com/business/2010/apr/01/net-porter-massenet-richemont.

Net-A-Porter's unrivaled selection, Net-A-Porter website, www.net-a-porter.com/intl/home.nap?channel=INTL&country=DE.

The basics of Net-A-Porter's service, Net-A-Porter website, www.net-a-porter.com/intl/home.nap?channel=INTL&country=DE.

There is a stylist on hand, "Personal Shopping Kicked Up a Notch", Katherine Rosman, The Wall Street Journal, December 3, 2013, http://online.wsj.com/news/articles/SB10001424052702304854804579236223551507130.

From the start, Net-A-Porter, "Net-a-Porter in campaign tie-up with Stella McCartney", Jenni Baker, M&M Global website, September 19, 2012, www.mandmglobal.com/news/19-09-12/net-a-porter-in-campaign-tie-up-with-stella-m.aspx.
&
"McQ Alexander McQueen Exclusive to Net-a-Porter", Reem and Natalya Kanj, Five Five Fabulous blog, May 17, 2012, www.fivefivefabulous.com/2012/05/17/mcq-alexander-mcqueen-exclusive-to-net-a-porter/.

The site gets around 6 million, "Net-a-Porter Names Magazine", Julia Neel, Women's Wear Daily, September 5, 2013, www.wwd.com/media-news/print/net-a-porter-names-magazine-7115095.

P. 117:

The expenditure on "off-price", Luxury Goods Worldwide Market Study 2011 (10th Edition), October 2011, Altagamma Foundation, Bain & Company, p. 11.

Some Balmain jeans sell out, Author's personal observation.

Multi-brand online shops such as Germany's, "Luxus im Netz", TextilWirtschaft, Sabine Spieler, www.textilwirtschaft.de.

The e-commerce site was launched, "About Us", Moda Operandi website, www.modaoperandi.com.

After only its first year, "Fashion Web Start-Up Raises $36 Million", Evelyn M. Rusli, Dealbook/ New York Times website, June 8, 2012, http://dealbook.nytimes.com/2012/06/08/fashion-web-start-up-raises-36-million/?_r=0.

P. 118

Under the guidance of, "Burberry's Angela Ahrendts: High tech's fashion model", Beth Kowitt, Fortune, CNN Money website, June 5, 2012, http://tech.fortune.cnn.com/2012/06/05/burberry-angela-ahrendts/.

Burberry was founded, Burberry website, "Heritage", http://uk.burberry.com/heritage/#/heritage/heritage-1800-1.

When Ahrendts took over in 2006, "Burberry's Angela Ahrendts: High tech's fashion model", Beth Kowitt.

To supplement the new direction, "Burberry's Angela Ahrendts: High tech's fashion model", Beth Kowitt.

It was one of the first, "Burberry launches commerce-enabled iPad application", Luxury Daily, Kaitlyn Bonneville, September 15, 2010, www.luxurydaily.com/burberry-streams-fashion-week-live-enables-ecommerce-via-ipad-app/.

Starting with its autumn 2010, "Fall 2010 Ready-To-wear Burberry Prorsum", Sarah Mower, Style.com/, February 22, 2010, www.style.com/fashionshows/review/F2010RTW-BURBERRY.

Customers were also encouraged; "Burberry's Angela Ahrendts: High tech's fashion model", Beth Kowitt.

The site also featured images, Art Of The Trench website, collaborations, http://artofthetrench.com/#.

Burberry's new business strategy, "Burberry Opens an Innovative London Flagship", Tina Gaudoin, Architectural Digest, December 2012 issue, www.architecturaldigest.com/ shop/2012-12/burberry-london-flagship-store-regent-street-article.

Salespeople carry iPads, "Burberry Opens an Innovative London Flagship", Tina Gaudoin.

Customers can also order items, "Burberry Opens an Innovative London Flagship", Tina Gaudoin.

P. 118 & 121:

Barbara Rybka, who spent, "Would You Buy Gucci Off Your Smartphone?", Kelsey Campbell-Dollaghan, Fast Company website, March 8, 2013, www.fastcodesign.com/1672019/would-you-buy-gucci-off-your-smartphone.

P. 121

Half of Gucci.com's traffic, "Would You Buy Gucci Off Your Smartphone?", Kelsey Campbell-Dollaghan.

After the launch of a new mobile site in early 2013, Gucci's shoppers have proven her right.

Their mobile conversion rates have increased by 70 percent, and mobile revenue has quadrupled.

Says Mark Lee, former CEO of Gucci, Erste Deutsche High End Fashion Studie (in German), Roland Berger Strategy Consultants, 2008, p. 96.

In fact, more than one-quarter, 2013 Digital Influence Report, Technorati Media, 2013, slide 16, http://de.slideshare.net/truthdefender/technorati-2013-digital-influence-report.

That number is even higher in China, where online shoppers put their trust in blogs, "Luxury Without Borders: China's New Class of Shoppers Take on the World", McKinsey & Company, p. 28.

Promoting a brand through personality, OscarPRGirl, http://oscarprgirl.tumblr.com.

Under the moniker OscarPRGirl, "Behind the Tweets: Learning from the Best of the Fashion Twitterati", Imran Amed, The Business of Fashion, January 12, 2011, www.businessoffashion.com/2011/01/bof-exclusive-behind-the-tweets-learning-from-the-best-of-the-fashion-twitterati.html.

P. 121 & 125
She quickly accumulated a six-figure, OscarPRGirl, Twitter, https://twitter.com/OscarPRGirl.

P. 125
It was launched by Christopher Parr, "Luxury Marketing and Social Media", Alison Rebecca, Pursuitist website, http://pursuitist.com/luxury-marketing-and-social-media/.

"There is a shortage of online…", "Luxury Marketing and Social Media", Alison Rebecca.

"Plenty of cold bling sites…", "Luxury Marketing and Social Media", Alison Rebecca.

"That's the void,…", "Luxury Marketing and Social Media", Alison Rebecca.

Followers of the website get, Pursuitist website, http://pursuitist.com.

CHAPTER SIX

P. 136
"Smaller streets boast…", "Luxury's New Destination: Neighborhood Streets Beckon Retailers And Investors", Laura Pomerantz, Forbes, December 4, 2012, www.forbes.com/sites/laurapomerantz/2012/12/04/luxurys-new-destination-neighborhood-streets-beckon-retailers-and-investors/.

"The stores have more…", "Luxury's New Destination: Neighborhood Streets Beckon Retailers And Investors", Laura Pomerantz.

Tom Ford's second Paris store, "Second Parisian store for Tom Ford", Di Marta Casadei, Vogue Italia website, December 19, 2012, http://www.vogue.it/en/trends/shop-in-the-shops/2012/12/tom-ford-opens-in-paris.

Luxury-store architect Peter Marino, "Fashion's shadow art world", The Financial Times, Vanessa Friedman, January 25, 2013, http://blogs.ft.com/material-world/2013/01/25/fashions-shadow-art-world/?.

P. 137
Says Piaget CEO Philippe Leopold-Metzger, "Piaget Sees China Sales Slowing as Stronger Yuan Boosts Travel", Bloomberg News, April 28, 2013, http://www.bloomberg.com/news/2013-04-28/piaget-sees-china-sales-slowing-as-stronger-yuan-boosts-travel.html.

Above its Bond Street store, "Louis Vuitton New Bond Street Maison", Ilvoelv.com, May 2010, www.ilvoelv.com/2010/05/louis-vuitton-new-bond-street-maison.html.

The concept of a private shopping apartment, "Louis Vuitton Elevates Exclusivity for Top Customers", Red Luxury, Red Luxury website, November 28, 2011, http://red-luxury.com/brands-retail/louis-vuitton-elevates-exclusivity-for-top-customers.

Although the exclusive spaces, "Louis Vuitton Elevates Exclusivity for Top Customers", Red Luxury.

P. 138
Infographic: Colliers Global Retail Highlights Report 2013, www.colliers.com/en-gb/uk/insights/property-news/2013/1008-global-retail-highlights-report-2013.

P. 139

Vuitton has perfected, Louis Vuitton website, store locator, www.louisvuitton.eu/front/#/eng_E1/
Stores/Store-Locator/Point-of-sale/Louis-Vuitton-Singapore-Marina-Bay.

P. 142

A number of brands, "Luxury stores pop up in hotels for inauguration", Hadley Malcolm,
USA Today, January 17, 2013, http://www.usatoday.com/story/money/business/2013/01/17/
inauguration-pop-up-stores-hotels/1839787/.

Consider the The Mall at Short Hills, "Luxury Shopping Malls Thriving: Taubman Sees Rising
Sales, While Kmart, Sears Cut Back", Alice Hines, Huffington Post, February 13, 2012,
www.huffingtonpost.com/2012/02/13/luxury-shopping-malls-taubman_n_1272882.html.

There is also the Beverly Center, "Luxury Shopping Malls Thriving: Taubman Sees Rising Sales,
While Kmart, Sears Cut Back", Alice Hines.

P. 142 & 143

Hermès itself only recently opened, "Luxury Shopping Malls Thriving: Taubman Sees Rising Sales,
While Kmart, Sears Cut Back", Alice Hines.
&
Short Hills Mall website, store directory, www.shopshorthills.com/directory.

P. 143

"High-quality regional malls…", "Luxury Shopping Malls Thriving: Taubman Sees Rising Sales,
While Kmart, Sears Cut Back", Alice Hines.

P. 144

"Location-based services must be…", PSFK Future of Retail Report 2011, summary slide 31, PSFK,
July 31, 2011, http://de.slideshare.net/PSFK/psfk-future-of-retail-report-2011-preview.

Statistics show that 67 per cent; "Why are fitting rooms so awful",
Elizabeth Holmes, Ray A. Smith, Wall Street Journal website, April 6, 2011,
http://online.wsj.com/news/articles/SB10001424052748703806304576243184005228532.

Restaurants are trying out flat-screen tables, E-Table website, E-Table™,
www.e-table-interactive.com/benefits/benefits-overview.html.

P. 145

It must be noted that the future of tax-free; "Online sales tax bill moving ahead in U.S. House",
Reuters, Reuters website, September 12, 2013,
www.reuters.com/article/2013/09/12/usa-tax-online-idUSL2N0H820Q20130912.
&
"Foreign tax collectors threaten to ensnare internet sellers with "virtual" nexus",
Alistair M. Nevius, J.D., CGMA Magazine website, September 25, 2013,
www.cgma.org/Magazine/News/Pages/20138804.aspx.

Certainly, the rapid growth of online, "Online retail sales continue to soar",
StockMarketWire.com, Stock Market Wire website, October 8, 2013,
www.stockmarketwire.com/article/4683290/Online-retail-sales-continue-to-soar.html.

"As the Internet creates…", "Temples Of Luxury: How Premium Brands are Using Brick
and Mortar to Maintain Exclusivity", Laura Pomerantz, Forbes website, June 18, 2012,
www.forbes.com/sites/laurapomerantz/2012/06/18/temples-of-luxury-how-premium-
brands-are-using-brick-and-mortar-to-maintain-exclusivity/.

"Bricks-and-mortar has become…", "Temples Of Luxury: How Premium Brands are Using
Brick and Mortar to Maintain Exclusivity", Laura Pomerantz.

P. 146

The accent on the "e", "On The Wings Of Céline", Suleman Anaya, The Business of Fashion,
March 27, 2013, www.businessoffashion.com/2013/03/on-the-wings-of-celine.html.

The brand, acquired by LVMH, "Phoebe Philo and Her Disciples", Benjamin Seidler, New York Times website, March 1, 2012, www.nytimes.com/2012/03/02/fashion/02iht-rphoebe 02.html?adxnnl=1&pagewanted=all&adxnnlx=1386337389-glKU3JVaHraoH/cK9CCHUA.

Philo had been pursued , "On The Wings Of Céline", Suleman Anaya.

Philo, previously successful as, "On The Wings Of Fashion", Suleman Anaya.

Next, LVMH shut down 20 of the 100, "LVMH Wipes Céline Slate Clean, Opening Way for 'Phoebe Effect'", Rachel Dodes, Christina Passariello, March 9, 2010, http://online.wsj.com/news/articles/SB10001424052748703954904575110010639056770.

Furthermore, the company pulled, "LVMH Wipes Céline Slate Clean, Opening Way for 'Phoebe Effect'", Rachel Dodes, Christina Passariello.

Her sleek, simple and refined aesthetic, "Phoebe Philo and Her Disciples", Benjamin Seidler.

Philo introduced recognisable designs, "On The Wings Of Fashion", Suleman Anaya.

"I felt it was necessary…", "LVMH Wipes Céline Slate Clean, Opening Way for 'Phoebe Effect'", Rachel Dodes, Christina Passariello.

"Now that we are establishing…" "LVMH Wipes Céline Slate Clean, Opening Way for 'Phoebe Effect' ", Rachel Dodes, Christina Passariello.

The efforts to recreate Céline's image, "LVMH Wipes Céline Slate Clean, Opening Way for 'Phoebe Effect' ", Rachel Dodes, Christina Passariello.

Trousers for €1,000, "LVMH Wipes Céline Slate Clean, Opening Way for 'Phoebe Effect' ", Opening Way for 'Phoebe Effect' ", Rachel Dodes, Christina Passariello.

P. 147:
This combination enamoured shoppers to the brand, even as the company decided to forego branching out into the lucrative e-commerce sector, "On The Wings Of Céline", Suleman Anaya.

In fact, since Philo arrived, "On The Wings Of Céline", Suleman Anaya.

Following the opening of a Céline flagship, "On The Wings Of Céline", Suleman Anaya.

While LVMH does not reveal, "On The Wings Of Céline", Suleman Anaya.

Confirming his decision to hire her, "On The Wings Of Céline", Suleman Anaya.

CHAPTER SEVEN

P. 156
In the desert of New Mexico, Virgin Galactic website, www.virgingalactic.com.

For $250,000: Virgin Galactic website, vehicles, www.virgingalactic.com/overview/spaceships/.

The extravagant suborbital flight, Virgin Galactic website, http://www.virgingalactic.com.

P. 157:
According to one study, about half, "Well-Heeled Shoppers Speeding Up Shift from Products to Experiences in the Global Luxury Market", press release, Boston Consulting Group, June 5, 2012, www.bcg.com/media/PressReleaseDetails.aspx?id=tcm:12-107201.

And that spending is growing, "Well-Heeled Shoppers Speeding Up Shift from Products to Experiences in the Global Luxury Market", press release, Boston Consulting Group.

The future of luxury marketing, "Climbing Mount Everest is Work for Supermen", New York Times, March 18, 1923, http://select.nytimes.com/gst/abstract.html?res=FA0717F83D 5416738DDDA10994DB405B838EF1D3.

P. 158:
Infographic: The Peninsula Hotels website, www.peninsula.com.

Rolls-Royce fleet, www.peninsula.com/moments/en/Hong_Kong/short_films.html.

Peninsula Signal 8 yacht, "The Peninsula Hotels Takes to the Ocean Waves with 'Peninsula Signal 8' Racing Yacht", Hospitality & Tourism website, The Peninsula Hotels, September 1, 2012, www.hospitalityandtourismdaily.com/news/asia-pacific/the-peninsula-hotels-takes-to-the-ocean-waves-with-peninsula-signal-8-racing-yacht.php.

F. Bigler: Peninsula Hotels website, hotel executives, www.peninsula.com/New_York/en/About_Us/Hotel_Executives/default.aspx?p=1.

P. 159:
The Peninsula Hotel chain, The Penninsula Hotels website, Penninsula Hotels press release, http://news.peninsula.com/EN/the-peninsula-hotels-takes-to-the-ocean-waves--with-peninsula-signal-8-racing-yacht/s/44af4d2b-f1d0-4c50-9be8-131a204efdaa.

For instance, Coldwell Banker Previews International, "How Agents Market And Sell Multi-Million Dollar Homes", Zillow, contributor, Forbes website, June 28, 2013, www.forbes.com/sites/zillow/2013/06/28/how-agents-market-and-sell-multi-million-dollar-homes/.

Bugatti, for example, www.bugatti.com/en.

Travel on every level, Visa Global Travel Intentions Study 2013, Visa, pp. 5 & 18.

That discrepancy is likely to, Visa Global Travel Intentions Study 2013, Visa, p. 5 & 18.

Those on a budget prefer booking online, Visa Global Travel Intentions Study 2013, Visa, p. 13 & 18.

P. 160:
National Geographic also taps its experts, National Geographic Expeditions, why travel with us?, www.nationalgeographicexpeditions.com/why.
&
National Geographic Expeditions, sustainable travel, www.nationalgeographicexpeditions.com/why/sustainable-travel.

Como Shambhala resorts play up the eco, Como Hotels and Resorts website, environments & community, www.comohotels.com/environments-community.

"Hotels today must know…", "Einchecken und wohlfühlen", Klaus Sendlinger interview, Markus Albers, (translated from the German) Brand Eins, August 2013, p. 119, www.brandeins.de/archiv/2012/nichtstun/einchecken-und-wohlfuehlen.html.

"Our goal is to actually make…", "Einchecken und wohlfühlen", Markus Albers.

P. 161:
Infographic: Visa Global Travel Intentions Study 2013, Visa, pp. 5, 18 & 21.

LVMH has kicked off its new ultra-luxury hotel, Cheval Blanc Clourcheval website, www.courchevel.chevalblanc.com/en/travel-diary/history.html.
&
Cheval Blanc Maldives website, http://randheli.chevalblanc.com/en.

The Italian luxury company operates, Bulgari Hotels & Resorts website, Bali, Bulgari Hotels & Resorts Bali, www.bulgarihotels.com/en-us/bali/the-resort/overview.

Bulgari also owns, Bulgari Hotels & Resorts website, http://www.bulgarihotels.com.

P. 162:
"We've now got a psychic…", "Einchecken und wohlfühlen", Markus Albers.

"Of course, you can only…", "Einchecken und wohlfühlen", Markus Albers.

"There are plenty of…", "Einchecken und wohlfühlen", Markus Albers.

Companies such as Docastaway, Docastaway website, what do we offer?, www.docastaway.com/pages/whatweoffer.

Four Seasons hotels cater to children, Four Seasons Hotels and Resorts, Maui at Wilea website, www.fourseasons.com/maui/services_and_amenities/family_at_four_seasons/family_travel/.

The Waldorf Astoria in Naples, Waldorf Astoria Naples website, www.waldorfastorianaples.com/Resort-Activities/Kids-Club.

And there are the Atlantis resorts, Atlantis Bahamas website, kids activites, www.atlantis.com/kids/kidactivities.aspx.
&
Atlantis Dubai website, things to do, www.atlantisthepalm.com/thingstodo.aspx.

P. 163:
Red Carpet Kids in Manhattan, Red Carpet Kids website, http://redcarpetkidsnyc.com/party.php.

The philosophy behind their parties, Red Carpet Kids website, http://redcarpetkidsnyc.com/party.php.

The content varies – improvisation lessons, Red Carpet Kids website, http://redcarpetkidsnyc.com/party.php.

All come with a customised cake, Red Carpet Kids website, http://redcarpetkidsnyc.com/party.php.

Alfred Dunhill has embraced, Alfred Dunhill London website, the homes, http://www.dunhill.com/the-homes/london/.

The label finds extraordinary, Alfred Dunhill Shanghai website, the homes, www.dunhill.com/the-homes/shanghai/.

P. 163 & 164
The company schedules themed, Alfred Dunhill website, day 8, http://www.dunhill.com/day8/.

P. 164
Several stores such as Merci, Merci website, about Merci, www.merci-merci.com/en/the-company.html.

"There is a marketing goal ultimately," says Patrizio di Marco, "Gucci CEO claims philanthropy gives meaning to luxury product", Tricia Carr, Luxury Daily website, June 6, 2013, www.luxurydaily.com/gucci-ceo-philanthropy-gives-meaning-to-luxury-products/.

"Definitely the long-term goal, …", "Gucci CEO claims philanthropy gives meaning to luxury product", Tricia Carr.

HON Circle members, Lufthansa Miles and More website, Hon Circle virtual tour, www.miles-and-more-promotion.com/honcircle.com/tour/index.html.

Members get a special luggage tag, Lufthansa Miles and More website, Hon Circle virtual tour.

To qualify, customers must, Lufthansa Miles and More website, Hon Circle virtual tour.

The scheme surrounds members, Lufthansa Miles and More website, Hon Circle virtual tour.

P. 165
"I want to be recognised …", "Einchecken und wohlfühlen", Klaus Sendlinger interview, Markus Albers, Brand Eins, p. 118.

"And when I come back, …", "Einchecken und wohlfühlen", Markus Albers.

"I do not need …", "Einchecken und wohlfühlen", Markus Albers.

"Most people …", "Einchecken und wohlfühlen", Markus Albers.

"But if I arrive with my dog …", "Einchecken und wohlfühlen", Markus Albers.

American auto enthusiasts, BMW website, European delivery, www.bmwusa.com/Standard/ Content/Explore/Experience/EuropeanDelivery/default.aspx?from=/Standard/Content/Explore/ Experience/EuropeanDelivery.aspx&return=/Standard/Content/Explore/Experience/ EuropeanDelivery.aspx.

After ordering a Porsche, Porsche website, European delivery, www.porsche.com/usa/ eventsandracing/europeandelivery/.

Porsche is also now building, "Porsche Breaks Ground On New U.S. Headquarters, Includes Test Track", Kurt Ernst, Motor Authority, November 28, 2012, www.motorauthority.com/ news/1080725_porsche-breaks-ground-on-its-new-american-headquarters.

Bugatti does this with its "atelier", Bugatti website, www.bugatti.com/en/tradition/history/molsheim.html.

P. 168
When Nick Jones opened the first Soho, "Soho House refinances", James Quinn, The Telegraph website, October 19, 2013, www.telegraph.co.uk/finance/newsbysector/ retailandconsumer/leisure/10391169/Soho-House-refinances.html.

There are branches in, Soho House website, houses, www.sohohouse.com/venues/houses.

CHAPTER EIGHT

P. 178
When LVMH announced plans in 2001, "Code of Conduct", Group Communications Department, LVMH, January 2001, LVMH website, pp. 4 & 11, www.lvmh.com/uploads/assets/Le-groupe/Documents/CodeofConductDEF.pdf.

By signing up for the UN initiative, United Nations website, United Nations Global Compact, www.unglobalcompact.org/aboutthegc/thetenprinciples/.

P. 179
In 2012, PR house Edelman discovered that 63 per cent, Edelman good purpose study 2012 (in German), Edelman, slide 13, www.slideshare.net/EdelmanInsights/zusammenfassung-ergebnisse-der-5-edelman- goodpurpose-studie-2012?smtNoRedir=1s.

That is a steep jump, Edelman good purpose study 2009, Edelman, slide 16, http://de.slideshare.net/EdelmanInsights/2009-goodpurpose-global-findings?from_search=4 & Edelman good purpose study 2010, Edelman, slide 15, www.slideshare.net/edelmanireland/ good-purpose2010globalppt-webversion?from_search=5.

And 63 per cent are willing, Edelman good purpose study 2012, Edelman, slide 7.

Nearly half of all people surveyed, Greendex 2012: Consumer Choice and the Environment – A Worldwide Tracking Survey, National Geographic & Global Scan, July 2012, p. 180, http://images.nationalgeographic.com/wpf/media-content/file/NGS_2012_Final_Global_ report_Jul20-cb1343059672.pdf.

In 2004, Gucci began, "Gucci announces the launch of worldwide eco-friendly initiative aimed at reducing paper consumption and Co2 emissions", press release, June 5, 2010, Kering website, www.kering.com/en/press-releases/gucci_announces_the_launch_of_ worldwide_eco-friendly_initiative_aimed_at_reducing#sthash.aryXgocU.dpuf.

In 2010, it not only introduced, "Gucci announces the launch of worldwide eco-friendly initiative aimed at reducing paper consumption and Co2 emissions", Kering press release.

It eliminated plastic, "Gucci announces the launch of worldwide eco-friendly initiative aimed at reducing paper consumption and Co2 emissions", Kering press release.

It has the Forest Stewardship Council certify, "Gucci announces the launch of worldwide eco-friendly initiative aimed at reducing paper consumption and Co2 emissions", Kering press release.

Its mannequins are made, "Gucci announces the launch of worldwide eco-friendly initiative aimed at reducing paper consumption and Co2 emissions", Kering press release.

P. 179 & 180
There are its Green Carpet Challenge handbags, Eco-Age website, Green Carpet Challenge, www.eco-age.com/green-carpet-challenge/.

P. 180
The handbags now, "A New Frontier for Sustainable Style", Jenny Greenwell, August 6, 2013, Eco-Age website, www.eco-age.com/a-new-frontier-for-sustainble-style/.

The company also has sunglasses, "Gucci biodegradable liquid wood sunglasses", Andrea Chin, Designboom, www.designboom.com/design/gucci-biodegradable-liquid-wood-sunglasses/.

Then there is its Sustainable Soles, Gucci website, Gucci sustainable soles, www.gucci.com/us/worldofgucci/articles/sustainable-soles-marona-green-ballerinas-california-sneakers.

"We have done a lot…, "Gucci: Sustainable Luxury at its Finest," Urbantimes.com, Elizabeth Keach, May 21, 2012, http://urbantimes.co/magazine/2012/05/gucci-sustainable-luxury-at-its-finest/.

In 2009, Gucci parent company Kering (formerly PPR), "Yves Saint Laurent announces its participation in PPR Group's Home project", Kering press release, April 2009, www.kering.com/sites/default/files/sites/default/files/press-release/YSL.pdf.

The company financed showings of the film "Home", "Yves Saint Laurent announces its participation in PPR Group's Home project", Kering.

P. 180 & 182
The succesful "vegan" company, Stella McCartney website, sustainability questions and answers, www.stellamccartney.com/experience/en/stellas-world/sustainability/sustainability-questions-and-answers/.

P. 182
But they also admit, Stella McCartney website, company statement, www.stellamccartney.com/experience/en/stellas-world/sustainability/company-statement/.

The demand has also created opportunities, Eco-Age website, Green Carpet Challenge, www.eco-age.com/green-carpet-challenge/.

Loro Piana, the 200-year-old Italian, Loro Piana, who we are, www.loropiana.com/flash.html#/lang:en/our_story.

The company has set up shop in Ulan Bator to monitor its wool production and make sure that it follows ethical animal husbandry rules among tribal herdsmen, Loro Piana, what we do, www.loropiana.com/flash.html#/lang:en/our_story.

P. 183 & 184
Nanai takes the skins left over, Nanai website, product, www.salmo-leather.de/en/produkt/manufakur/.

P. 184
The company uses exclusively organic, Nanai website, product, www.salmo-leather.de/en/produkt/manufakur/.

Nanai takes its name from, Nanai website, manufacture,
http://www.salmo-leather.de/en/produkt/manufakur/

Watches were (and are), Patek Philippe website, values,
www.patek.com/contents/default/en/values.html.

Porsche is happy to proclaim, "Porsche: every day sporty driving fun", Porsche press release,
Porsche website, May 16, 2012, www.porsche.com/usa/aboutporsche/pressreleases/pag/
archive2012/quarter2/?pool=international-de&id=2012-05-16.

P. 184 & 185

"People read something in The New York Times…", "New Year's Resolutions", Lucie Greene,
Sphere website, 2013, www.spherelife.com/future-trends/.

P. 185

"They read the wallets…", "New Year's Resolutions", Lucie Greene.

"They think it is all made in China.", "New Year's Resolutions", Lucie Greene.

"It's in the interest of…", "New Year's Resolutions", Lucie Greene.

"From a business perspective, …", "Green: The New Color of Luxury", Grail Research,
December 2010, p. 14, www.grailresearch.com/pdf/ContenPodsPdf/2010-Dec-Grail-Research-
Green-The-New-Color-of-Luxury.pdf.

"For example, energy conservation…", Green: The New Color of Luxury", Grail Research.

"Our business has grown…", Green: The New Color of Luxury", Grail Research.

"We are able to achieve…", Green: The New Color of Luxury", Grail Research.

Along with the rise of sustainable products, 1.618 Sustainable Luxury website,
http://guide.1618-paris.com/home.

One of the most high profile, Tesla Motors website, about, www.teslamotors.com/about.

P. 186 & 187

The International Organisation for Standardisation, ISO website, http://www.iso.org/iso/home.html.

P. 187

ISO has developed the 14000 family of, ISO website, ISO 14000,
www.iso.org/iso/home/standards/management-standards/iso14000.htm.

ISO then has other standards under the 14000 heading, ISO website, ISO 14000.

Most companies would help, Forest Stewardship Council website, https://ic.fsc.org/.

Tourism companies, Global Sustainable Tourism Council website, www.gstcouncil.org
&
Sustainable Travel International website, http://sustainabletravel.org.

Restaurants can also look for, Marine Stewardship Council website,
www.msc.org/?set_language=en
&
LEED website, www.usgbc.org/leed.

P. 188

Founded in 1997, SAI website, who we are,
www.sa-intl.org/index.cfm?fuseaction=Page.ViewPage&pageId=490.

The organisation says, "About SAI", SAI PDF download, http://sa-intl.org/_data/n_0001/
resources/live/SAI_brochure_2012.pdf.

Compliance should be, "About SAI", SAI PDF download.

P. 189

And he comes with a serious pedigree, Honest By website, Bruno Pieters www.honestby.com/en/page/92/bruno-pieters.html.

The experience affected him so profoundly, Honest By website, Bruno Pieters.

Next to Pieters' designs, Honest By website, designers, http://www.honestby.com.

Consumers can not only choose among, Honest By website, http://www.honestby.com.

Besides, the company only, Honest By website, about, www.honestby.com/en/page/16/about.html.

It is an all-round concept, Honest By website, about.

CHAPTER NINE

P. 199

"You need to be trustworthy.", Interview with Milton Pedraza, Markus Albers.

"You need to be caring.", Interview with Milton Pedraza, Markus Albers.

"That is very hard to do but that is the differentiator…", Interview with Milton Pedraza, Markus Albers.

P. 199 & 200

"You can measure it in customer…", Interview with Milton Pedraza, Markus Albers.

P. 201

"Luxury Brand Marketing to Wealthy Millennials", The Luxury Institute, 2011.

P. 202

Especially in the bricks-and-mortar, Luxury Retail Management: How the World's Top Brands Provide Quality Product and Service Support, Michel Chevalier, Michel Gutsatz, John Wiley & Sons, March 2012, chapter 3.

"The competitive advantage is…", "Luxury Institute exec: Humanize first, mobilize second", Rimma Kats, Mobile Marketeer website, October 16, 2012, www.mobilemarketer.com/cms/news/strategy/13998.html.

The company recently discovered, "Audi boosted brand loyalty 7.5pc by redefining employee experience", Erin Shea, Luxury Daily website, June 26, 2013, www.luxurydaily.com/audi-boosted-brand-loyalty-7-5pc-via-redefining-employee-experience/.

Audi based the dealership programme, "Audi boosted brand loyalty 7.5pc by redefining employee experience", Erin Shea.

It then invited more than, "Forrester's Harley Manning: Audi of America Revs Up the Customer Experience", Harley Manning, 1to1 Media website, June 21, 2013, www.1to1media.com/weblog/2013/06/audi_of_america_revs_up_the_cu.html.

The company's strong US sales, "Audi sets 4th straight U.S. sales record with a month to spare on November 2013 gains", Audi website, news, December 3, 2013, www.audiusanews.com/pressrelease/3631/98/audi-sets-4th-straight-u.s-sales-record-month.

"Our goal was to redefine…", "Audi boosted brand loyalty 7.5pc by redefining employee experience", Erin Shea.

P. 202 & 203

"We had to redefine the employee experience…", "Audi boosted brand loyalty 7.5pc by redefining employee experience", Erin Shea.

P. 203

Audi's customer loyalty, "Audi boosted brand loyalty 7.5pc by redefining employee experience", Erin Shea.

Robbie Williams once sang, "Something Beautiful", Williams Robert Peter, Guy Anthony Chambers, published by Lyrics © Universal Music Publishing Group, EMI Music Publishing.

P. 206

Again, it is not rocket science, "7 steps to inspiring luxury customers' loyalty", Richard Dixon, Luxury Daily website, October 9, 2012, www.luxurydaily.com/7-steps-to-inspiring-luxury-customers'-loyalty/.

"Recognition of their loyalty…", "7 steps to inspiring luxury customers' loyalty", Richard Dixon.

P. 209

The Ritz-Carlton only, The Ritz Carlton website, exclusive partnerships, www.ritzcarlton.com/en/Rewards/RedeemingRewards/ExclusivePartnerships/Default.htm.

Customers can even gain points, The Ritz Carlton website, earning rewards, www.ritzcarlton.com/en/Rewards/EarningRewards/Default.htm.

The programme has also introduced, The Ritz Carlton website, elite benefits, www.ritzcarlton.com/en/Rewards/EliteBenefits/Default.htm.

P. 211

Link only works through Google, Tiffany created a "True Love" campaign "Tiffany What Makes Love True", Rebecca Thomson, Retail Week website, February 3, 2012, www.retail-week.com/tiffany-what-makes-love-true/5033260.article.

This created an emotional bond, Tiffany & Co., Facebook, https://www.facebook.com/Tiffany.

"I challenge the luxury brands…", "Luxury Customer Experience Needs To Evolve", Jeannie Walters, 360 Connext website, November 29, 2012, http://360connext.com/luxury-experiences-up-luxury-goods-down/.

"Create intimacy. Reward the…", "Luxury Customer Experience Needs To Evolve", Jeannie Walters.

P. 212

Within the automotive sector, 2012 New Luxury Vehicle Loyalty Study, Polk/Auto Trader.com, p. 2, PDF download, www.weworkforyou.com/files/insights/pdf/2012NewLuxuryVehicle LoyaltyStudy-NADASINGLEPAGES.pdf.

With cars, two things are vital, 2012 New Luxury Vehicle Loyalty Study, Polk/Auto Trader.com, p. 3.

P. 214

Mercedes-Benz buyers, 2012 New Luxury Vehicle Loyalty Study, Polk/Auto Trader.com, pp. 3 & 4.

BMW drivers appreciate the company's image but also want performance from their sedans, 2012 New Luxury Vehicle Loyalty Study, Polk/Auto Trader.com, pp. 3 & 4.

It was mostly for brand reasons, "The Volkswagen Phaeton to Attempt Successful Rebirth in U.S. Market", Joseph Choi, NADA website, July 30, 2013, www.nada.com/b2b/NADAOutlook/UsedCarTruckBlog/tabid/96/entryid/280/The-Volkswagen-Phaeton-to-Attempt-Successful-Rebirth-in-U-S-Market.aspx.

Women remain loyal, "New Study from Polk and Autotrader.Com Reveals Top Reasons Luxury Buyers Stay Loyal", Polk website, February 3, 2012, www.caranddriver.com/features/2014-volkswagen-phaeton-future-cars.

For Bugatti this is all in sync, "After a Brief Revival Maybach Brand Falls Back Into Retirement", Noah Joseph, JustLuxe website, August 20, 2012, www.justluxe.com/lifestyle/luxury-cars/feature-1811979.php.

P. 214 & 215

And the 24/7 concierge service,
"Notruf für Luxuskunden", Peter Weyer, Stern.de website, November 8, 2002,
www.stern.de/auto/autowelt/maybach-notruf-fuer-luxuskunden-338611.html.

P. 216

Lufthansa's elite, Hon Circle web tour,
www.miles-and-more-promotion.com/honcircle.com/tour/index.html.

Fashion house Lanvin, "Valentino Sells VIP Perks With Handbags Amid Slowdown",
Andrew Roberts, Bloomberg News, January 24, 2013, www.businessweek.com/news/
2013-01-24/gucci-sells-vip-perks-with-handbags-to-counter-slowdown.

A handbag made from, "Valentino Sells VIP Perks With Handbags Amid Slowdown",
Andrew Roberts.

Only 14 were made – a number that says, "You, the customer, are special to us",
"Valentino Sells VIP Perks With Handbags Amid Slowdown", Andrew Roberts.

For instance, a select handful of, "My Gucci Addiction", Buzz Bissinger, GQ website, April 2013,
www.gq.com/news-politics/newsmakers/201304/buzz-bissinger-shopaholic-gucci-addiction.

A fitting for a custom-made. "My Gucci Addiction", Buzz Bissinger.

Smaller tokens of, "My Gucci Addiction", Buzz Bissinger.

P. 217

The brother of, Mr Porter website, www.mrporter.com.

PICTURE CREDITS

ABOUT THE AUTHORS

Dr Martin C. Wittig

is a Senior Partner and Chairman of Roland Berger Switzerland. He lives in Herrliberg near Zurich. Dr Wittig was global Managing Partner and Chief Executive Officer of Roland Berger Strategy Consultants from 2010 to 2013. He is a visiting lecturer at the University of St. Gallen and was elected to the university's International and Alumni Advisory Board. Dr Wittig and his wife Susanne are also involved in multiple social and cultural organisations, such as Ashoka Switzerland, Right to Play, the Swiss Institute for Art Research and the Museum of Photography in Winterthur.

Dr Fabian Sommerrock

is a Principal and member of the management team of Roland Berger Switzerland. From 2011 until 2013 he was Executive Assistant CEO and before a Project Manager at Roland Berger Strategy Consultants. Dr Sommerrock is an expert in strategy development, transformation, post-merger integration and reorganisation as well as efficiency and change management. He is a visiting lecturer at the University of St. Gallen with a focus on marketing, and a Director of the AlpEuregio.BusinessClub, a non-profit organisation.

Philip Beil

joined Roland Berger Germany in 2003, and is a Partner in the Consumer Goods and Retail Competence Center and heads the Fashion and Luxury Practice Group. He is the author of various studies and articles about the luxury goods and fashion markets. Previously, he was Director of Business Development for an international start-up company that he co-founded. Philip is a graduate of Ludwig-Maximilian University and lives with his wife in Munich.

Markus Albers

is a journalist, entrepreneur and writer of non-fiction books. He lives in Berlin, Germany. Markus is a Managing Partner at content marketing agency Rethink as well as Contributing Editor for *Monocle* and *Brand Eins*. His work has also been published in *GQ, Architectural Digest, Vanity Fair, Der Spiegel, Stern, SZ-Magazin, Welt am Sonntag* and *Die Zeit*. His books, *Meconomy*, and the business book bestseller *Smart Work*, received enthusiastic reviews and have been translated into many languages. He also speaks and gives keynotes based on the books' topics.